PRAISE F

MW01097047

"Reading *The Storied Church* is like reading a good storybook. Matt Gorkos writes *about* story, *in* stories, and *for the sake of* renewing the living stories of congregations. Churches will find inspiration and guidance here as they seek to understand and transform their communities in relation to new challenges. Readers will delight in the lyrical, imagistic language and will find much to deliberate in the explanations of stories and story-making. Thanks to Gorkos for a fine interweaving of theological insights, probing questions, and practical guidance for congregations."

—Mary Elizabeth Moore, dean emerita and professor of theology and education, Boston University School of Theology, and author of *Teaching as a Sacramental Act*

"*The Storied Church* is a welcome oasis in the weary US mainline church landscape. From *The Big Lebowski* to Alcoholics Anonymous to his own participation in a UCC ministry laboratory in Pennsylvania, Matt Gorkos engages and articulates a twenty-first-century theology of story for a church too often stuck in the twentieth. It's way past time for mainline US Christian churches to claim our own particular and powerful story, and then tell it well. Every council, vestry, presbytery, or governing body should read this book. And then dream new dreams, together."

—Jason Chesnut, pastor in the Evangelical Lutheran Church in America since 2010, itinerant preacher, freelance filmmaker, and biblical storyteller working at the edges of institutional Christianity

"In this bold and insightful project, Matthew Gorkos diagnoses the problem facing mainline churches as an existential crisis tied to their loss of communal identity, rather than merely declining membership rolls. Drawing from Scripture, narrative theology, cinema, and twelve-step programs, Gorkos offers story-based resources for authentic church renewal."

—Rebecca L. Copeland, assistant professor of theology, Boston University School of Theology

The
Storied
Church

The
Storied
Church

A Strategy for
Congregational Renewal

Matthew Gorkos

FORTRESS PRESS
MINNEAPOLIS

THE STORIED CHURCH
A Strategy for Congregational Renewal

Copyright © 2021 Fortress Press, an imprint of 1517 Media. All rights
reserved. Except for brief quotations in critical articles or reviews, no
part of this book may be reproduced in any manner without prior written
permission from the publisher. Email copyright@1517.media or write to
Permissions, Fortress Press, PO Box 1209, Minneapolis, MN 55440-1209.

Unless otherwise cited, the Scripture quotations are from New Revised
Standard Version Bible, copyright © 1989 National Council of the
Churches of Christ in the United States of America. Used by permission.
All rights reserved worldwide.

Cover image: 1194721796 © fona2 | iStock
Cover design: Marti Naughton (sMart desigN)

Print ISBN: 978-1-5064-7009-2
eBook ISBN: 978-1-5064-7010-8

To my parents—Kirk and Nancy—
who nurtured in me an abiding love
for both the church and stories

To my children—Ezra, Soren, and Josephine—
for the ceaseless joy it brings me to
watch your stories unfold

Contents

Figures

Preface

A Brief Story on Writing This Book

> *Let me read with open eyes the book my*
> *days are writing—and learn.*
>
> —Dag Hammarskjold, *Markings*

I have two loves rooted deep in my heart, the seeds of which I do not remember being planted—the love of church and of story. Although I cannot identify a particular moment when either of these loves took shape, I can look back over thirty-five years of a life that bears witness to the transformative potential of both. I am who I am today because of the role that the church and story have had in shaping me. They are the reason I became a pastor. They are the reason the stack of books to read on my nightstand is never low and my DVD collection is always too full. They are the reason I can rarely go a whole conversation without making some obscure allusion to a favorite movie or television character. They are the reason that when I read Scripture, I picture it in my mind's eye with the same cinematic detail as though the Coen brothers had directed it. They are the reason for this book. But for most of my life, those two loves have existed mostly independently of one another.

I believe in the church—in the power of faithful people serving a good and gracious God—and I believe in the power of a good story. Moreover, I believe, as this book will argue, that church and story—harnessed together—could be an even more powerful force for goodness in our world.

If not for this deep love and commitment to church and story, I would not have staked my doctoral work and my future in ministry on proving the claim that the revitalization of our dying churches rests in the hands of story. But I have reason to be confident. Time and time again, I have been personally reminded of story's ability to draw us in and discover places we didn't know we longed to see, parts of ourselves we didn't know we had hidden away, and feelings we didn't know were being stifled. Stories invite us into spaces where we can grapple with fear and doubt and where we can taste joy and hope, not in escapist retreat but in a way that restores us and renews our hearts and minds for facing our world and whatever experiences and challenges life throws at us. This is why humanity has always turned to stories to express our deepest questions and longings. We are storytelling animals.

Neuroscientists, anthropologists, archaeologists, and psychologists all agree. Story is how our brains and our communities make sense of things. I listened to an entire audiobook on a recent seven-hour drive home from vacation in which the author approached the human propensity for story from an evolutionary standpoint and concluded that we have told and will continue to tell stories because, in some way, storytelling helps us survive.[1] Storytelling helps us cope with change and loss. Storytelling helps us impart lessons and life skills to the next generation. As human beings, it seems we can't do without story.

This book—this whole idea of story-centered church renewal—was birthed out of my suspicion that the restorative, transformative, life-giving function that stories have for us as individuals may serve the same function for communities of faithful people. If stories help us survive as human creatures, why can't they help churches survive? Yet most people in our pews and most pastors have neither the time nor the desire to study the neuroscience or psychology suggesting the storiedness of our brains. Likewise, story-centered renewal seeks to draw from the wisdom of science in conversation with narrative, practical, and (to an extent) process theologies in order to put forth an accessible ecclesial vision for how a local congregation might harness the combined power of church and story.

Much of this book was written over the course of 2019 as the culminating piece of my doctoral work through Boston University. I am thankful for the guidance and patience of the faculty there, especially my advisor Dr. Rebecca Copeland, and the program director, Dr. Eileen Daily. I am also grateful for the open ears, open minds, and encouragement of my colleagues—particularly, Nathan, Axel, Jon, Linda, Lisa, David, and Jeff—who endured what must have often sounded like mad ramblings as I tried to formulate these ideas into something more coherent. The writing process, as it so often can be, was disjointed and sporadic—interrupted along the way by life's happenstance. But eventually, it was completed, submitted, and approved.

However, in the time between completing that original version of the work and returning to it in order to revise and bring it to this present form, so much else has happened in my life and in the world around me—namely, a global pandemic. The coronavirus has impacted individuals, families, and our country in ways that time will only continue to reveal. But it has significantly impacted our local churches too, many of whom have had to close their buildings and scramble to rethink entire ministry models that had taken for granted the privilege of physical presence. In many ways, the challenges posed by the coronavirus exposed my own assumptions of a church's ability to gather in person and that assumption's influence on the idea of story-centered renewal.

However, what sustains my conviction that story-centered renewal is an important idea and may yet be an invaluable tool to our churches is the way in which the coronavirus has exponentially compounded the existential dread of dying churches. Like the way Camus had observed disaster bringing the worst of society's underlying fears to the surface, this plague has cast a harsher light on the fear lurking in our churches. Congregations who had already been concerned over finances and weekly giving saw that anxiety skyrocket when worship services had to be canceled and online giving was not an established practice. Congregations who had already been worried about dwindling attendance saw it suddenly drop to nearly zero. Congregations who had put so much of their pride and passion into hosting community meals and social events were now unable to safely do so and were left wondering what, if *anything*, they could do. In other words, the coronavirus may have changed the way churches were doing ministry, but it didn't change the problem that I am naming at the start of this book—the despair of the declining churches. It actually made it worse. The problem story-centered renewal seeks to remedy has only become more prevalent and more urgent in the age of coronavirus. Our churches need hope now more than ever that it will not always be a desperate scramble to survive.

Because even when the coronavirus is finally controlled enough to return to some sense of normalcy, which I'm hoping by the time you're reading this it has, new challenges will emerge. The world is constantly changing. Life is constantly happening. And every time something changes, the church must figure out how to respond to the adaptive challenges. Certainly, many churches have answered the challenges posed by the coronavirus with creative approaches to online worship, fellowship, and giving. Also, many churches have shifted their mission attention to health and hunger concerns directly related to the pandemic. However, the lasting tenability of making any creative changes and maintaining the energy of the congregation to continue them depends on the degree to which those things that began as temporary alternatives are able to be integrated and reconciled with the overall identity and ministry of the church. Story-centered renewal offers a framework for retaining what has proven good and true to the congregation by aligning it not as the result of desperate scrambling but as a faithful expression of who the church is in response to its present circumstances and to the needs of its community. In that way, story-centered church renewal is an adaptive resource that a congregation can use to navigate and respond to each new challenge, whenever and whatever that challenge may be.

In chapter 1, I identify the basic adaptive challenge that story-centered renewal is attempting to address along with why story and narrative are ideal psychosocial tools for meeting that challenge. In chapter 2, I begin the merging of church and story by demonstrating the storied quality of the Christian faith and how story-centered renewal is biblically and theologically faithful. In chapter 3, I move from theological to ecclesiological terms and explore the communal benefits of story-centeredness and how they might impact congregational life. In chapter 4, I pull in the insights of storied thinking marketing, communication, and business experts in order to suggest several tips and cautions for discerning a church story. Finally, in chapter 5, I present a practical overview for implementing story-centeredness in your church.

I write this from a pastor's perspective, hoping to encourage and empower other pastors and lay leaders with both the hope and the tools they need to effect revitalizing change in their faith community. As you will read, much of the testing of the ideas behind story-centered renewal occurred while I was ministering among the wonderful people at Pennsburg United Church of Christ (PUCC), to whom I am forever indebted for their gracious hospitality, for their patient trust in my leadership, for their support and willingness to give my weird, untested ideas a fair shot, and for their unfailing love for their church. Thank you, PUCC, for sharing your story with me.

Last, thank you to the church leaders who are reading this. Thank you for caring enough about your church to dedicate your time and money to learning how you can help. It is my hope in the pages that follow that by sharing with you the power of story and its impact on a local mainline church like PUCC, you might be inspired by what truth you find and what parallels you see with your own community. To help in this regard, I have included questions for reflection at the close of each section so that you can connect what you are reading to your own church context. It is my hope that you'll come away from this book with a renewed appreciation for story and a fresh understanding of how story's power applies to the life of faith and ministry.

Wherever you are in your story—wherever your church is in its story—it is my prayer that by God's grace your next chapter would be blessed.

Matt Gorkos
September 1, 2020

Church in Search of Story

The Village Church

Once upon a time, there were village churches. Out of a combination of resolute piety, yearning for fellowship, and central location, these churches emerged as the spiritual and social hearts of their respective communities. (If you didn't just read that in your best epic-rolling intro voice—like the one you use at the beginning of *Star Wars* movies—go back and read it again with some dramatic flair.) Once upon a time, *not* in a galaxy far, far away, but right here in America, village churches were being founded in New England by pious pilgrims, in Pennsylvania and New York by devoted Reformed and Lutheran Germans, and all throughout the rural countryside by fervent Methodist circuit riders. "Once upon a time in America, Protestant congregations were village churches that offered weary immigrants a new home in a new world."[1] These words of Diana Butler Bass bear the slightest tinge of wistfulness. Yet when she wrote them in 2006, she was not setting out to paint a fairy-tale picture of yesteryear. Rather, she was offering a sobering reminder that the twenty-first-century socioreligious landscape in America threatens the continued existence of those same Protestant congregations and their denominational support systems. Villages are ceasing to be villages; and consequently, the village churches that once occupied a central place in the spiritual and social lives of their citizens are facing rapid institutional decline and death. She writes later in the same book, "The old Protestant mainline is no longer mainline. It no longer speaks from a pinnacle of cultural privilege and power."[2] The world and our local communities have changed—and with them, the place of the mainline church.

For example, I recently had the privilege of serving for three years at a small United Church of Christ (UCC) congregation in southeastern Pennsylvania whose institutional journey fits the village church pattern—and current dilemma—of many mainline congregations. The origin story of Pennsburg United Church of Christ (PUCC) opens in Germany around the turn of the eighteenth century, where after enduring decades of warfare and strife, citizens began deciding by the thousands that their homeland was no longer hospitable to farming or habitable for living. Therefore, many made the risky decision to cross the Atlantic in hopes of better land and a more stable political and religious environment. For most of them, the destination was a territory known then as "Penn's Woods." After arriving in Philadelphia, the German newcomers would follow the Delaware River northward into areas now comprising Montgomery, Northampton, Lehigh, and Bucks counties.[3] Wherever they found suitable land, they settled and began farming. Wherever groups of farms developed, communities took shape and villages sprang up. Wherever villages developed, there arose a desire for organized spiritual care and social connectivity.

However, due to a severe shortage of ordained clergy, these communities would regularly enlist respected, literate citizens to read Scriptures and sermons to them. Enter into the story John Phillip Boehm, a schoolteacher and devout Reformed Christian, who had emigrated from Germany in 1720. Boehm, though not ordained, was asked by several local faith communities to not only read to them but also organize worship and administer the sacraments. Over the course of his ministry, Boehm would help establish a dozen of these small, village congregations in southeastern Pennsylvania.[4] Over the next fifty years, these village congregations (and many others) were organized under a governing authority that became the Reformed Church in the United States.[5] Finally, in 1840, shortly after the next wave of German immigrants began to arrive in America, the church in Pennsburg was born.

For the next 117 years, it ministered to its community as Pennsburg Reformed Church. When the United Church of Christ was formed in 1957—the German Reformed Church being one of the four converging branches—the church adopted the title of the new denomination. Today, over 175 years since its founding, the church endures—still tracing its legacy back to Boehm's village ministry model, still situated on the border of Montgomery and Bucks counties, and still perched on a Main Street corner in Pennsburg, Pennsylvania. It is a church built upon a foundation of close-knit local community, familial legacy, and its German Reformed tradition.

Once upon a time, PUCC was a thriving village church. However, the taken-for-granted characteristics of village life that had contributed to the sustained institutional well-being of the church throughout much of the nineteenth and twentieth centuries have either waned considerably or disappeared completely. Like many suburban towns, Pennsburg and its surrounding area have undergone such rapid change over the last fifty to sixty years that it is no longer accurately called a "village."[6]

Once upon a time, PUCC was a village church, but not anymore. Although its physical location has not changed, its context for ministry has. The town still exists, but many of its "village" qualities have disappeared. As the firm foundation upon which the church was built has been shaken and weakened by increased isolationism, impermanence, and historical discontinuity, it has experienced the institutional decline shared by many of its fellow churches within mainline American Protestantism. And so I want to highlight those three trends, which directly contradict the foundational values of PUCC and are having a costly impact on innumerable mainline congregations.

Since 1960, Pennsburg's population has increased 125 percent, a growth most visibly evidenced by the continual conversion of local farmland into housing developments. In other words, new people are moving into town, but they are moving mainly into new houses on the outskirts of the community. Ironically, as the population of Pennsburg has increased and new homes are being built closer in proximity to one another, the residents have actually grown more relationally distant from one another. In village life, citizens would intentionally venture from the seclusion of their farms and homes in an effort to connect with their neighbors. The opposite is now the case: following busy workdays or long commutes, citizens intentionally choose seclusion and disconnection. No longer a place where everyone knows everyone, Pennsburg has become a town where neighbors are content to coexist as strangers.

Sociologists and theologians alike have lamented this suburban trend toward isolationism as a key contributor to the atrophy of authentic community. In 1989, Ray Oldenburg decried the loss of neighborhood connectivity and advocated for the formation of "third places," which would foster belonging, relationships, and a communal identity.[7] Likewise, twenty years later, Peter Block recognized an innate human need for belonging and stressed the importance for any given community to encourage relationships and cohesion among its citizens.[8] The social fabric of the village is no longer knitted so tightly.

The way in which the close-knit village has been unraveled by isolationism cannot be denied nor can its impact on the village church be minimized. The village church once attracted new members based solely on its reputation as the local center of both religious and social life in the community—on its ability to sew relationships. Long-standing residents of the village attended for fellowship, be that fellowship sacred or secular in nature. New residents of the village came to get connected, both spiritually and socially, with their new neighbors. In some cases, the occasion for gathering was literally to knit. Knitting or quilting groups were once a hugely popular staple of mainline/village church life. However, the church is no longer the center of village life, and the knitting groups have largely gone the way of the church's role as the town knitter of community. On one hand, those who crave community can now choose from a veritable marketplace of options, including professional networks, niche interest clubs, youth and intramural athletics, and groups at the nearby YMCA. On the other hand, the overall desire for that community has waned. Due to isolationism, the once cherished status of the village church as the hub of the close-knit community formation has been emptied of its value.

Another foundational element of village life and of the village church is an enduring familial legacy. "The health of old mainline denominations was for many decades reliant upon the health of their mostly small rural and often kinship-constituted congregations."[9] People and families would settle and stay for generations. Parents would raise children in the church, and those children would then raise their children in the church. Marriage and baptism were two major avenues—more like boulevards—of membership growth. However, this legacy has also been undermined, in Pennsburg and elsewhere, as marked increases in mobility, educational opportunities, and distances between home and the place of employment have all contributed to the disruption of village familial patterns. Today, parents are having fewer children, and the children they have are more likely to pursue higher education. Consequently, more children are leaving home, leaving town, settling down, and starting their families in places other than where they grew up. Stephen Compton argues, "Disruption in the pattern of family perpetuation of membership has led to critical changes in these once extraordinarily stable congregations."[10] Village churches once built their membership and based their programs and ministries on an assumption of proximity and progeny. New members came naturally, and evangelism was rather effortless. As Linda Bergquist and Allan Karr state, "These churches stop needing to find people because so many people find them."[11] For so long, mainline churches took for granted the steady regeneration of membership. However, once people stopped finding them (or stopped looking), those same churches find themselves ill equipped to begin reaching out.

Last, the original village church at Pennsburg was richly rooted in the specific immigrant experiences and German culture of its members. Even as generations passed, there continued to be a shared heritage among those who held dearly to their German ancestry. In fact, PUCC is only forty years removed from Sunday morning sermons being delivered twice—once in English and once in Pennsylvania Dutch—and its liturgical style and worship are still reflective of its German Reformed tradition. Its heritage is also evident in the congregation's customary celebrations. For instance, Harvest Home Sunday is recognized in worship on the last Sunday of September each year and traces its origins to the annual thanksgiving for another fall crop harvested and stored. The German heritage is also still apparent in its food. PUCC's collective appetite is for such beloved German culinary staples as sauerkraut, pickled red beets, and pot pie. Those connections to German tradition have less significance in Pennsburg today. Though the town's population growth has led to little in terms of racial diversity, it has diluted the German influence on Pennsburg's local culture. Whereas the residents were once predominantly of German descent, only one-third of the town's residents still trace their roots to German ancestry.

These three factors have undoubtedly helped precipitate the decline of the village church. As is the case with many mainline churches, the symptoms of decline at PUCC have been most observable in shrinking membership rolls, worship attendance, and endowment funds. Over time, these societal trends of isolationism, impermanence, and historical discontinuity have functionally handcuffed their ministry by simultaneously contributing to the depletion of human and financial resources and rendering many of its programs and models for ministry irrelevant in light of the changes to its setting. Still, in the face of its decline, it is a church that, like many of our churches, holds on to the hope of renewal.

Questions for Reflection

- How did your church come into being? What is its origin story?

- How has your church's context changed over the last fifty years? Twenty-five years? Five to ten years?

- In what ways do isolationism, impermanence, and historical discontinuity impact your congregation?

The Existential Crisis

The knee-jerk response for many struggling churches is to address threatening symptoms by haphazardly siphoning waning resources into one of the three societal trends I mention above or hastily investing in gimmicks promising temporary reprieve. Many church renewal strategies emphasize stewardship campaigns or evangelism programs that seek to address particular aspects of decline without addressing the larger concern. Further, I maintain that focusing too narrowly on the signs and symptoms is like band-aiding a bursting dam. It causes churches to settle too quickly for superficial cures while failing to see the true magnitude of a problem that is existential in nature or failing to identify real potential for change. As the pillars of the "village" have been eroded by a combination of isolationism, impermanence, and historical discontinuity, the proverbial rug has been pulled out from under the village church.

By way of illustration, the 1998 cult comedy The Big Lebowski is a convoluted goofball caper featuring Jeff Bridges, John Goodman, bowling, and an abundance of f-bombs.[12] The film follows the erratic journey of the Dude, played by Bridges, as he is thrust into a web of confusing criminal activity involving a greedy millionaire, a trophy wife, a reclusive daughter, a gang of nihilists, a porn producer, and a rival bowling team.

One might justifiably wonder, "What does a film like that have to do with church renewal?"

There's not a literal connection. But there is a metaphorical one.

One of the film's brilliant ironies is that although his character is first introduced to the viewer as distinctively calm and laid back, the Dude is, for most of the film, anything but calm or laid back. Instead, he regularly appears flustered, confused, and prone to emotional outbursts, all the while grasping for some sense of understanding or control of the situation in which he finds himself. At one point, when he has reached peak disequilibrium, he groggily mutters, "All the Dude ever wanted was his rug back." This clues the viewer in to the true source of the conflict his character endures.

The plot of the story is set into motion when the Dude's beloved rug—the one that "really tied the room together"—is ruined by two bumbling henchmen. The desecration of the rug, in addition to his best friend Walter's goading, instigates the Dude's quest for a replacement. His desire to find a new rug is the only reason he gets caught in the tangled web of confusion. The rug that tied it all together is removed, and suddenly the Dude's whole sense of self and way of being begin to come unwound. Ultimately, the Dude's problem is neither with nihilists nor with the other Jeffrey Lebowski; his problem is an existential one. His experience with the rug has bowled over his fundamental trust in a world that is as peaceful and nonaggressive as he is. The missing rug is a metaphor for the subversion of the central belief that made sense of the Dude's life and world.

Likewise, the mainline church's conflict is not primarily against external opponents such as youth sports programs, other neighborhood churches, millennials, or secularists. It's much closer to our hearts and souls. Once upon a time, there were village churches, but the villages have changed. Now, without the sure status and mission as the village church, mainline congregations are left searching for a raison d'être—a clear justification for our existence and importance to the work of God—for a sense of meaning that undergirds all that we do. This loss of the "village" has resulted in the church suffering not merely from financial and membership decline but also from an institutional despair—a prolonged sense of ecclesial aimlessness and spiritual malaise.[13]

With its rug gone missing, the church needs something to tie it all together. It needs a new way of centering its congregational and organizational life so that the incongruities it is currently experiencing between its beliefs and the world around it can be addressed not with "desiccated abstractions and scatological immediacies" but rather in a way that is substantial and lasting.[14] That something substantial and lasting to tie it all together is story. A story is to the church what the rug is to the Dude. It's not the wall-to-wall red carpeting that ties the room together; it's a church's story that staves off despair. A church that has lost its story is a church that has lost connection to its identity and its way of being. With the story of the village church no longer ringing quite true to the mainline church's ministry or peoples' experience, our churches must turn the page to discover the next part of the story.

Church renewal means overcoming the fear and despondency caused by the disappearing story. "The opposite of being in despair," writes Kierkegaard, "is believing."[15] The path to renewal is a path of rediscovery leading to a belief in the identity and purpose of the church and its unique, exciting, and essential contributions to the work of God in the world. Renewal means searching for and finding a congregational story to tie it all together. Renewal means attending to and answering the existential questions at the heart of the problem: "Who are we? Why are we here?"

Near the turn of the twenty-first century, Diana Butler Bass had already begun observing symptoms of what she terms a "nomadic existence" and their debilitating effect on mainline churches—symptoms like radical individualism, aimlessness, consumption, fragmentation, and forgetfulness.[16] Yet she had also noticed that not all mainline Protestant churches were suffering. Some, in spite of the societal trends, were thriving. They were growing in terms of membership, financial stability, and spiritual maturity. So in 2002, she set out to study what, if any, common strategies or key characteristics these thriving churches possessed that other struggling churches did not.

What she discovered was that while there were very few programmatic likenesses, each of the congregations had undergone a similar soul-searching transformation process: "Whether threatened by spiritual boredom or facing church closure, each congregation asked two questions that sparked deep change: Who are we? What is God calling us to do? They discovered a renewed sense of identity and clear purpose in serving the world. They experienced a change of heart that transformed their communal understanding of who God had made them to be."[17] The healthy, thriving—formerly village—churches shared no other secret aside from a common attentiveness to and reckoning with the respective existential struggle they each faced.

A decade after she began her investigation into thriving mainline churches, Bass wrote *Christianity after Religion*, in which she observed how, over those ten years, society had continued to shift away from institutionalized forms of spirituality. Nevertheless, her remarks about healthy congregations echo the conclusions of her earlier work: "Churches with a clear sense of who they were and what they were called to do were more vibrant than those with a muddled identity."[18] And she suggests that it is still incumbent upon churches to be asking, "Who are we in God?" and "Who is God through us?" if we want to survive and sustain an uplifting and active spiritual environment in a postmodern, postdenominational, poststructural world. She concludes that book by describing a new sort of approach to mainline Protestant vitality "marked by its insistence on connection, networks, relationship, imagination, and story instead of dualism, individualism, autonomy, techniques, and rules."[19]

I am neither surprised that she lists imagination and story among the key ingredients to congregational renewal and life nor surprised that she juxtaposes them against rules. In fact, I will argue that the storying imagination is even more crucial than she supposes. Why? Because the essential existential questions churches must be asking—"Who are we?" and "What are we doing here?"—are best, most frequently, and perhaps only answerable in the form of story. Thus the existential crisis—the ecclesial aimlessness and spiritual malaise plaguing the mainline church—may be rightly understood as a shortcoming of its storying imagination. If any congregation means to replace the rug that has been pulled out from under it and tie its room back together, it must refine its central belief about who it is in God and who God is through it, and to do so it must learn to think in terms of story and tell a story about itself.

Questions for Reflection

- Where do you see signs of "aimlessness and spiritual malaise" in your church?

- Who is your church in God?

- What is God calling your church to do?

Storied Existence

Having defined the existential nature of the problem and pre-scribed story as the appropriate remedy, this section aims to explain *why* I believe that story is the key to overcoming the exis-tential despair of our mainline congregations. My argument stems from the assertions of narrative thinkers who propose that human beings make sense of our lives in story form. This is summarized by narrative psychologist Dan McAdams: "In the narrative mode of thought, we seek to explain events in terms of human actors striv-ing to do things over time."[20] I believe the life of a congregation can be explained similarly. Therefore, because of its influence, and in order to further explore the function of story and establish a foun-dation for its use in church renewal, it is necessary here to discuss the contributions of two seminal figures within narrative thought.

French philosopher Paul Ricoeur has literally written the book(s) on narrative and time. Of story's essential role in making coherent sense of life, he writes, "It 'grasps together' and integrates into one whole and complete story multiple and scattered events, thereby schematizing the intelligible signification attached to the narrative taken as a whole."[21] In other words, a storying imagina-tion organizes otherwise disparate life experiences into a narrative plot in order to ascribe to them a singular meaning. Whenever new experiences challenge the meaning, the story is revised to maintain coherency. This suggests that mainline churches need not entirely forsake their origin stories and totally reinvent themselves but rather that we must revise our stories to make coherent meaning of our new experiences.

The storying imagination strives not only for coherence but also for continuity. A narrative view of experience looks beyond the present moment in seeking to connect it to what has been (past) and what will be in time (future). For Ricoeur, this function of story fulfills a deep existential need: "I see in the plots we invent the priv-ileged means by which we re-configure our confused, unformed, and at the limit mute temporal experience."[22] And since histori-cal discontinuity is one of the three major disrupters of modern mainline church stability, it warrants paying close attention to the way in which story interacts with history.

In narrative thought, history is understood not as fixed and factual but rather as a flexible, subjective piece of the whole story and thus is capable of being rethought and understood in new ways. As finite creatures, we can only view our past through the lens of our present, but "when the present changes, the good historian may rewrite the past."[23] Thanks to its flexibility, the past is constantly being reframed to bring a sense of continuity to the present and a trajectory to the future. McAdams describes the process this way: "We recast and revise our own life stories so that the past is seen as giving birth to the present and the future, and so that beginning, middle, and end make sense in terms of each other."[24] This notion of continuity ensures that as a village church grows into a new sense of story, that story will likely be a permutation of the village church, not a radical departure from it.

To describe the dynamic tension between humanity and time vis-à-vis the divine, Ricoeur draws heavily from the work of Saint Augustine. In considering the eternal nature of a holy God, Augustine faced the quandary of how a person bound by the constrictions of time could hope to encounter a God unbound by it. In his wrestling, Augustine pondered the concepts of past and future and posited that their only real existence occurs in the present. Ricoeur posits that for Augustine, the past exists only as past-present (or memory), and the future exists only as future-present (or expectation).[25] In that light, storytelling functions in the living moment as a practice that erects a bridge between memory and expectation. Ricoeur recognizes this bridge not only as horizontal across time but also as a vertical, sacred interplay between human limitations and eternal transcendence: "Time becomes human to the extent that it is articulated through a narrative mode, and narrative attains its full meaning when it becomes a condition of temporal existence."[26] In other words, because it acts as a bridge, story is both the mode by which the eternal assumes human flesh as well as the mode through which humanity can glimpse the transcendence of God. Story, by occupying that cruciform intersection, possesses a liminal power that cannot be found elsewhere.

Mainline churches today are in dire need of the bridge and the power that story provides. In many of our churches, tradition has long functioned as our bridge from the present to the past. However, tradition is rarely able to do the work of making a bridge to the future.[27] When our posture is predominantly backward facing, pining for the past and huddled against the headwinds of change, we are unable to see where God might be leading us. Moreover, without the vertical bridge by which traditions and rituals are connected through story to the divine, those rituals lose their spiritual meaning. If existential despair is the loss of life's meaning due to incoherent and discontinuous experiences, and if stories are the means by which people justify the brief, apparent insignificance of human life, then church stories will bridge the void by telling how and why its moment in time and place matters by connecting the church's existence to a larger Story.[28] By shaping past, present, and future into a story, individuals and churches might bring a cohesiveness to life that, because it transcends the living moment, connects to that eternal present—to the intersection of our time-bound stories with the Story of a God beyond time.[29]

In his assessment of Augustine, Ricoeur demonstrates how the formulation of narrative is an existential imperative for finding meaning in life. In his subsequent discussion of Aristotle, he attempts to define the mechanics of that narrative formulation by identifying three key components: the *poetic*, the *muthos*, and the *mimesis*.[30] The *poetic* component is the intent and the conscious creativity of one authoring the story. The *muthos* is the composition of the story into an organized system or structure. The *mimesis* is the implication that the story means or points to something larger than itself. In short, by incorporating both Augustine and Aristotle, Ricoeur defines narrative formulation as both an unconscious, instinctive human response to existential anxiety and a knowing, imaginative act of the human mind.

The storying of life experience lingers in the tension of spontaneity and intention. On one hand, storying is an instantaneous

reaction to lived experience, and on the other hand, it is a deliberate, creative enterprise. This simultaneous nature of narrative is
why I propose story to be a central tool in church renewal. Because
humans have been made with story-making brains, a church
of humans already possesses both a story and a collective storying
imagination, whether it knows how to use it or not. If the church
can become more aware of its innate desire to story experience, it
may become more deliberate in its storytelling, more focused on
articulating a story that answers the pressing questions of identity
and mission, and better equipped to speak of its congregational
life and ministry as having a single, divinely willed trajectory.

The second seminal figure whose ideas contribute to this
view of storied church renewal is Stephen Crites, who published
an influential article in 1971 titled "The Narrative Quality of Experience." In it, like Ricoeur, he argues that storytelling is a natural and
necessary tool with which to understand lived human experience
in relation to time. However, Crites's observations are of significant
benefit to story's application to church renewal because the asso-
ciation between temporal human stories and stories of a larger,
more transcendent scope receives specific treatment in Crites's
article, as does the tension between spontaneity and intent in story
formulation. Crites offers helpful categories and frameworks for
understanding the various levels of story present within the life of
any given church.

First, Crites differentiates between sacred stories and mundane stories. He uses the word *sacred* not as a distinctly religious
term but rather to signify a story's transcendent quality. Sacred
stories are those that form the context and backdrop for life. He
defines them as "stories that orient the life of people through
time, their life-time, their individual and corporate experience and
their sense of style, to the great powers that establish the reality
of their world."[31] Sacred stories are seemingly ethereal, in that,
as Crites suggests, they are told not by authors but by the culture itself. These are stories that the community often accepts as
unquestioned principles. For instance, a common sacred story of

many churches might concern the holiness of the sanctuary space and the reverence due to it when occupied.

Mundane stories, on the other hand, are more ordinary stories rooted in human experience. Again, in the way Crites uses it, *mundane* is not a derogatory term but rather a more literal reference to a story's down-to-earth quality. Mundane stories tend to reinforce or make relevant the sacred stories: "In order to initiate their children in 'the ways of the world,' parents tell them [mundane] stories."[32] Continuing the above example, one of the mundane stories used to reinforce the holiness of the sanctuary might star the rambunctious child whose horseplay resulted in the Christ candle's being toppled and broken.

Crites describes the relationship between mundane and sacred stories as having "distinction without separation."[33] Within that mutuality arises the question of changing the story: if a congregation is to refine its story, to which of these types of story should it turns its primary focus? And so it is important to notice the mutual dependency of sacred and mundane stories in that sacred stories form the world from which the mundane stories arise, while mundane stories serve as less mythic, more relatable variations of those sacred stories. Sacred stories are the abstract concept or ideal, while the mundane stories are the tangible, incarnated version.

In a stable system, there is a cooperative balance between sacred and mundane stories wherein they reinforce one another. However, if the sacred story changes, the mundane stories change to reinforce the new story. If a church would begin telling a sacred story that, in fact, a sanctuary is holy *because* it is a space that allows even for the most haphazard expressions of the church's youngest members, then the mundane stories might become examples of when the manic energy of children resulted not in disaster or disruption but in the joy of those who witnessed it.

The mundane stories always exist as stories within a sacred story. The question that their mutual dependency raises is whether influence can flow in the other direction too. Are mundane stories always subservient to the sacred story, or can they be subversive?

Can changing the mundane change the sacred? If, as Crites suggests, sacred stories are products of the culture as a whole, then the question raises the possibility of changing church culture from within through the telling of new mundane stories that challenge the status quo.

What are the mundane stories being told within the community of the congregation? What sacred stories do they reinforce or subvert? What are the sacred stories the church holds dear? What mundane or sacred stories need to change for the church to be renewed? Sometimes, the church possesses a valuable sacred story and yet needs better, more relatable and interesting mundane stories to reinforce it. Sometimes the church discovers an undercurrent of mundane stories that all contradict a certain sacred story that the church isn't prepared to admit needs changing. The interplay between mundane and sacred creates an ongoing internal tension for the church. The mutuality of the sacred and mundane as they interact to shape congregational culture requires that story-centered renewal attend not to one or the other type but rather to both sacred and mundane—to the overarching story and the stories within that story occurring at the ground level of our experiences. The church's story plays a sacred role inasmuch as who it believes God to be will shape the life of the congregation. The church's story also plays a mundane role inasmuch as it expresses the congregation's embodied understanding of who God is through its ministry.

Questions for Reflection

- What are some of the sacred stories at play in your church?

- What are some mundane stories supporting those sacred stories?

- What, if any, are the mundane stories contradicting the sacred stories?

Church in Search

The church's story occurs at both the mundane and sacred levels. A church's story is at once an expression *of* the church and a mold *for* it—two distinct but inseparable pieces of its storied existence. Yet whether spoken of in terms of mundane or sacred, the goal of the church's story is the same: resonance. Crites describes resonance as when a person hears a piece of music for the first time and genuinely feels moved because something in it connects with their own personal story.[34] The church in search of renewal is a church in search of a story that resonates.

The changes to the local community have pulled the rug from beneath the village church, resulting in its tangible institutional decline and less tangible descent into institutional despair. Yet it is human instinct to want to resolve the discordant sense of aimlessness and meaninglessness through the formulation of story. The church, too, may resolve its despair as it discerns and defines its story. The renewal of our mainline churches must begin with the search for the sort of story described in this chapter—a story that integrates past, present, and future coherently; that builds a bridge of continuity not only across time but also as a link between the transcendent scope of God's Story and the temporal experiences of human life, and that resonates in such a way so as to inspire new life within the church and spark new connections outside.

This bridge that story forms between church, God, and the surrounding community is not static. Professional storytellers often refer to the storytelling triangle to describe the dynamic relationship between a story, its teller, and the audience and how the three mutually affect one another. A similar triangle (see figure 1.1) can be used to illustrate the dynamics at play in the church story as it encapsulates the intersection of congregational identity, theology, and mission. In this model, the more familiar storytelling triangle is set within a larger triangle representing the factors impacting a church's story.

The church is the story's teller, but more than that, the church is a character in its own story. Therefore, the character circle encompasses the individual stories of church members as well as

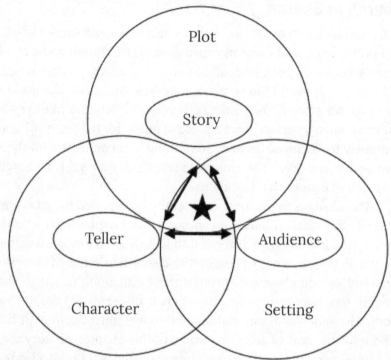

FIGURE 1.1. Church storytelling triangle

the history of the congregation itself. The characters of any worth-while story are never static. They change and grow. Likewise, as a result of the impermanence caused organically by membership losses and gains, the character of the congregation is not static. As the constituency of the congregation changes, a good church story will change with it.

The setting circle is the context for the story that includes the story's audience. When, where, and to whom is the story being told? As the setting changes, such as with the passing of time or how the town of Pennsburg has changed or even as there are dramatic shifts in the larger culture like the movement from modernism to postmodernism to post-postmodernism, the church story will change with it.

The plot, in terms of the church story, is God's Story. It is the overarching narrative in which the church understands itself as a participant and is embodied in both the words and practices by which the church proclaims the gospel. Even this circle does not remain unchanged in our churches (although some may argue it should). Rather, the plot can be altered as, through discerning prayer and faithful learning, the church's awareness of what God is doing in and through it grows and shifts. As the plot changes, the story will change with it.

Consequently, like the storytelling triangle, the church's story should never be static. There should always be a flow of responsiveness between character, setting, and plot, because if the church story is not allowed to change, discord and existential dread are inevitable. Few things are as insufferable as having to endure a story whose characters are unfamiliar, whose setting is totally foreign to the audience, and whose plot is dull or obscure. The story either will not be heard or upon being heard will be immediately forgotten. The church story must be dynamic and ever changing in order to remain resonant.

A resonant church story will connect with the members of the church, engaging their passions and gifts, and inspiring the investment of their time and resources into the ministry of the church. A resonant story, like the drummer in a march, provides a unifying sense of style and rhythm to church life. The church's story not only answers the existential questions of identity and mission; it involves its individual members in that story. They recognize the church's story as familiar—as representative of their own stories. In that resonance, the church's story offers a sense of identity and mission to individuals as well as the institution. It helps each person to feel a part of the whole.

A resonant church story will also connect with people outside its walls. As the church becomes clear on who it is in God and who God is through it, and as it begins to tell that story in word and deed, the story will ring familiar to those in its surrounding community. The hope is that the church's story will foster connections and build relationships where they did not previously exist.

This longing for resonance—the church's search for a story that can be heard in stereo with God's Story and can be heard by the world around it—makes the quest for story-centered renewal a deeply theological effort. Or, as Sallie McFague puts it, "The purpose of theology is to make it possible for the gospel to be heard in our time."[35] Both theology and story are after resonance. Thankfully, the search for story and the subsequent centering of that story in the life of a faith community do not start from a blank slate. There are stories and storiedness already present in the church, and not only because of the human propensity toward storytelling. Both the Christian faith and Christian community are innately storied, but that storiedness must be recognized and refined because our stories shape our behaviors as individuals and communities. Therefore, in the following two chapters, I will explore story-centeredness along two relevant theological avenues: *doxa* and *praxis*—belief and action.

Questions for Reflection

- Who are the characters involved in your church's story?
- What is the setting for your church's story?
- What does your church believe God to be doing?

A Storied Faith

In the Beginning Was Story

"In the beginning . . ." The elder pauses, sits, clears his throat as best he can of its gravelly phlegm, and readies himself for the telling of a lengthy story—one he learned when he was still a child, probably one as young as the little boy eagerly seated before him. The child has just asked, with a curiosity so pure as would only be accepted from a child, "What are we doing here?"[1]

"In the beginning," the elder commences, "the earth was formless, void, and shrouded in darkness. There was something, but at the same time, it was nothing. There was no rhyme or reason to it. But God's spirit hovered over the raging waters—over the chaos below. Finally, God spoke a word, and with that word and each successive word, God began harnessing the chaos and bringing order to all Creation."

The story continues being told so that by the time the elder has finished, the child will have been given an answer, albeit perhaps a different answer than he had expected because it is an answer in storied form, but an answer nonetheless to the original question of identity and purpose of existence. This is the beginning of faith, and it is a story because faith itself is storied. Faith, like story, aims to answer the deepest existential questions of humans and human communities.

The elder's story of the beginning satisfies the curiosity and sparks wonderment in that one child. Soon the child may return to hear the story a second time. Or maybe another child arrives to ask the same question, having heard the report of the elder's fascinating story. Eventually, the elder tells the story so many times that the whole village knows it by heart. As those children grow up, the wonderment of the story doesn't fade. When they have children of their own and those children start asking the same questions, the parents share the elder's story with them. When the future generations of that community are ripped from their homes and taken to a far-off place, struggling with doubt and despair, they remember and cling to the story of who they are and why they exist. The story helps tether them to something steady in the storm. Over time, the story is told so often and grows so familiar that it is written down as a treasured story of faith to be remembered, shared, and told by generations to come. That story of the beginning becomes the first story—the first words—in the peoples' sacred Scripture. From there, the storied faith becomes intertwined with the peoples' own story.

In this chapter, I aim to show how in the biblical witness, faith and story are inseparable. I will present the formation of Scripture as the work of the storying imagination, the product of a faithful people striving to articulate and maintain their identity and mission over time and in light of changing and challenging communal experiences. Biblical scholar and theologian Walter Brueggemann insists that since the beginning, story has been the primary mode of faith transmission. He warns, "Trouble surfaces in the community of faith whenever we move from the idiom of story."[2] Sallie McFague spells out the warning even more explicitly: "If theology becomes overly abstract, conceptual, and systematic, it separates thought and life, belief and practice, words and their embodiment, making it more difficult if not impossible for us to believe in our hearts and confess with our lips."[3] In other words, the faith of the Bible is a storied faith, and to lose the storiedness of that faith can seriously impact the way faith is understood and expressed in professing communities. Story-centered renewal is rooted in a conviction of story's critical role in the beginnings, development, and continuing vitality of the Christian faith.

Every church's story is a creative proclamation of its faith and declaration of its being. According to James Cone, "Every people has a story to tell, something to say to themselves, their children, and to the world about how they think and live, as they determine and affirm their reason for being. The story both expresses and participates in the miracle of moving *from nothing to something, from nonbeing to being.*"[4] It is appropriate that Cone should have made such an observation, because it cannot be overstated the degree to which Black, feminist, womanist, queer, and other theologies of marginalized people have far more readily exhibited the storiedness of faith precisely for its affirmation of their being. For those whose right to exist is constantly questioned or threatened, the storied faith provides not only the language for belief but also the solid ground on which the community can stake a claim to life. Because the traditionally white mainline Protestant church has, until its recent decline, taken its continued existence for granted and endured very little in the way of threat, we would do well to learn from the collective wisdom of our siblings in faith for whom this struggle is far from new. They have already realized what the mainline is now discovering: to lose the storiedness of faith is to risk the continued existence of the community because it halts—or worse, reverses—that movement from nonbeing to being.[5] For a church to lose the storied faith and its storying imagination is to risk ultimately receding into nothingness and nonbeing. It is the path of the dying church.

Annette Simmons writes, "Stories hover over the facts and draw lines of connection or disconnection—good, bad, relevant, or irrelevant—to create meaning."[6] The similarity of imagery and message between Simmons's words, Cone's words, and those of Genesis 1:1–2 are striking. Stories, like the spirit of God, hover over what is something yet nothing until it can be given meaning and order. Yet not only have congregations suffered as the "facts" of their existence ceased to be held together in a coherent, meaningful way, but the vibrancy of peoples' faith has suffered too. As Cone suggests, "God's story becomes our story through the faith made possible by the grace of God's presence with us."[7] In the absence of storied faith, our connection to one another and our connection to God both suffer. It is no accident that the exodus from the pews that began in the middle of the twentieth century has coincided with the mainline church's shift away from a storied faith to faith as a system of information. I will suggest that, in many ways, twenty-first-century mainline American Christianity has lost the storiedness of its faith, and I will further suggest that there is a correlation between this loss and the churches' spiritual stagnancy and institutional decline.

Humanity's innate propensity for storying experience is a gift from the God whose words changed nothingness into something-ness. Our human appetite for creating and curating stories is a characteristic of the *imago Dei* in us.[8] Moreover, in addition to the care of God's creation, humanity has been entrusted with the care of the storying imagination. Yet since the beginning, since the serpent first made humans question their story by asking, "Did God really say . . . ?," the storying imagination has been under siege. As such, the secondary purpose of this chapter is to establish story-centered church renewal as not only an ecclesial need but also an urgently needed recovery of a foundational part of what it means to espouse the Christian faith.

Consider the central metaphor in the 1984 film *The Never-Ending Story*, in which looms The Nothing—a steadily creeping vacuum of darkness.[9] The film is a depiction of the death of story through the death of imagination. A critique of modern utilitarianism and rationalism, the film suggests that the realm of Fantasia is being engulfed by The Nothing due to the dwindling collective imagination of humanity, who no longer has hopes, dreams, or a love of stories. I suggest there is a Nothing that lurks and devours in the realm of faith as well.

Whereas I noted in chapter 1 that stories are often the best way to capture the truth of human experience, I posit that their effectiveness extends to the human spiritual experience. To lose the storying imagination is to lose a crucial part of faith. Fellow proponent of storied faith Norbert Haukenfrers asserts, "The pursuit of our rational obsession has led the modern church to give up on the storied imagination as the way of knowing truth, as there is no way of reconciling the paradox."[10] That is, because stories aren't considered true enough in a world that demands we only think in absolutes, Christians have buckled under the pressure of Enlightenment rationalism and abandoned the storiedness of faith. Prior to the above assertion, Haukenfrers had asked whether the realm of story was "one of the last sacred preserves of our imagination, untouched by the Enlightenment?"[11] If the institutional decline of American mainline Christianity is any indication, then that last bastion is crumbling quickly. We are witnessing The Nothing engulfing the church and the Christian faith through the death of imagination and story.

In the end, the fate of Fantasia depends on whether a young boy can accept that *he* is a participant in its story. In the climactic scene, when the characters from the story are desperately crying out for his input, the voice of his rational mind keeps insisting skeptically, "It's just a story; it's not real." A narrative mind will counter that rationalism by asserting, "There is only story."[12] The film's climactic moment captures the crisis facing many churches: Which mind will win the day, the rational or the narrative? Like that of Fantasia, the fate of the church depends on whether it can reignite its storying imagination and reclaim its storied faith, because the story of faith and of the church is a never-ending story of the same sort. Each one must hear the story's calling: "Each one of us must find our part and place in the great, good, never-ending story and then trust the story with our lives."[13]

Questions for Reflection

- Is the congregation's origin story generally well known to the people? Why or why not?

- How does your church's origin story find its genesis in God's will?

- How would you describe your congregation's imaginative abilities?

Story and the Still-Speaking God

A foremost piece of story-centered renewal is to understand the Bible as both a product of and tool for the development of a storied faith. In attending to the storiedness of Scripture, not only will the church learn *from* the stories of its ancestors in faith, but it will learn *how* those ancestors used stories to grapple faithfully with existential and epistemological crises. As we consider the biblical world at its various levels, such as "the world at the time of the story and the world at the time of the writing of the story," we may gain insights into reconciling faith with our world.[14] For example, in his book *The Creative Word*, the intent of which is to take the form and genre of the Old Testament canon as a model for biblical teaching, Brueggemann writes, "If we can understand how Israel dealt with these difficult matters of continuity and discontinuity, of stability and flexibility, we may . . . understand afresh how the Bible is the live Word of God."[15] In other words, although particular verses may not describe specific processes for story-centered community, the Bible itself is evidence that God's people have always turned to storied thinking in response to crises of identity and mission. So why shouldn't the church employ storied thinking in facing its challenges today?

As a local congregation within the United Church of Christ, PUCC is part of a denomination that understands itself as being located within the storying tradition of the Christian faith. One of the mottos of the United Church of Christ since the start of the twenty-first century has been the assertion that "God is still speaking." The phrase refers to the denomination's belief in a continuing testament, not in terms of an open biblical canon but in terms of a belief that the Holy Spirit continues to reveal God's will and word through Scripture, experience, the living tradition, and reason.[16] Within the framework of a continuing testament—a never-ending story, if you will—the composition of the Bible is suddenly seen from a new perspective. Rather than demanding some sort of univocal or singular message, Scripture is appreciated for its tensions and diversity because those differences attest to distinct authors and context and the livingness of their experiences in relationship to God. There is movement. The Bible reflects the on-going struggle of communities to understand and articulate their faith in light of an ever-changing world. By studying the Bible through a storied faith lens, the church may gain instructive wisdom into not only how it understands its own story but also how it imagines and articulates that story to share with others.

Just as there is a creative context to Scripture, there is likewise an interpretive context that is in constant flux as well. And it is when we fail to attend to the complexity and/or to the potential differences in either the creative or interpretive contexts that we risk concretizing an otherwise dynamic word. When we ignore the limitations of the particular perspective through which each of us approaches Scripture and faith, we risk absolutizing a single version of the story. In doing so, not only do we dismiss the perspectives of others, but our religious language can become idolatrous or irrelevant.[17] Sallie McFague describes this interpretive situation in a way that sounds quite similar to the storytelling triangle from chapter 1 (see figure 1.1): "The total interpretive situation of a text is a complex triad of speaker, text, and hearer in which many possibilities are present for misunderstandings, differences of opinion, varying interpretations, and revisions of previous interpretations."[18] And as with the storytelling triangle, changes to any element of the interpretive context necessitate theological consideration.

The idea is that every new experience necessitates reflection within the context of the storied faith. Whenever the situation or circumstances change, or whenever new information is discovered, the question must be asked, "Now, what does the past mean? What does Scripture mean?" Alasdair MacIntyre characterizes this question as that of an "epistemological crisis" and insists that the crisis of discovery or revelation does not require abandoning history and tradition but rather reflecting within the tradition and reconstituting that tradition to fit the new experience. In this way, the storied faith represents a "continuous reconstruction" of tradition.[19] When tradition goes on too long without being questioned or revised, it can become incoherent, irrelevant, or dead. Already in the early 1980s, McFague was lamenting a tradition gone stale: "For many of us the language of the Christian tradition is no longer authoritative; no longer revelatory; no longer metaphorical; no longer meaningful. Much of it has become tired clichés, one-dimensional, univocal language."[20] The storied faith resists the flattening and deadening of tradition. When we declare that God is still speaking, it is out of the conviction that the storied faith tradition of the church is alive, and what it means to be faithful is continually being challenged and refined by new experiences. As long as God's people continue to have new experiences, the people's story will continue to need to be revisited and revised.

Within narrative theology, the word for this evolution of story is *mythopoesis*. Mythopoesis seeks the resonance mentioned in chapter 1 by addressing the changes to interpretive contexts and relating the story in such a way that it is relevant to the present audience. In other words, mythopoesis does not call for a brand-new story but rather a new way of telling the story so that it is appropriate to the new circumstances or in light of the new experiences. It is storied faith "for the living of these days," as the hymn goes.[21] Mythopoesis is indicative of a Christian theology that "is always an interpretation of the 'Gospel' in a particular time and place."[22] Indeed, even the New Testament stories of Jesus—the four Gospel accounts—are told from different perspectives with different agendas because they are being told to different audiences facing different circumstances.

Furthermore, theologian John Navone goes so far as to suggest that mythopoesis is a mandatory practice of Christian faithfulness: "The stories which authentically Christian lives tell, both as individuals and [collectively] in the Church, constitute a living mythopoesis which represents, rehistoricizes, and relates the 'Gospel-truth' of the story God tells in Christ to the needs and interests of every generation. Each historical generation of Christians re-enacts and revitalizes in its own characteristic way the story which God tells in Christ."[23] In this regard, church renewal is a mythopoetic endeavor. For instance, the village church story no longer resonates and is no longer relevant to the situation or experience of PUCC, so the church must rehistoricize its story to relate it and the gospel to the needs and interests of a new generation and the new sort of community it occupies. The mythopoetic task of the local church is to ask and answer, "What does it mean to be a Christian community here, in this place, right now?"

Thankfully, the mythopoetic task has an instructive biblical precedent not only in the Gospels but in the Hebrew Scriptures as well. In examining the substance and structure of the Torah, Brueggemann argues, "Education in Israel is based on 'let me tell you a story'—not just any story, but this one which we have found reliable."[24] The Torah is a story-centered curriculum for teaching the next generations their peoples' history, identity, and mission. Moreover, it is the basis for storied faith and practice, as paraphrased from Deuteronomy 6:20–21a: "When your children ask you, 'What's the meaning of all we say and do?,' tell them the story." Beyond presenting the Torah as story centered, Brueggemann highlights several characteristics of story as it functions in the Torah and how it may function similarly in the formational practices of other faith communities. The characteristics he describes fit together to suggest that scriptural story is not meant to be universally prescriptive but rather descriptive of the way local communities of faith understand and engage in their world.[25]

The stories are localized in that they tell of characters and events located in specific places and times. They are also localized to the degree to which each story bears a provenance to the circumstances and community that produced it. In that organic particularity, there is a sense of connection and ownership that gives the stories greater value to the faith community than if the stories had been designed for a wider audience: "This is our story . . . not because it's the best story or the objectively true one but because it is ours."[26] I will say more in chapter 4 about the importance of a congregation's story having this particular, local flavor.

Stories help create a way of seeing the world. They are not meant to provide answers to every question for all time but rather to form a model for discerning answers in whatever time and place a community may exist at the moment. Stories shape our collective vision of the past and future and especially of the present. In that sense, the stories become timely metaphors of timeless truths—bridging the mundane/sacred boundary as only stories can do. Consequently, the Bible contains a plethora of metaphors that the communities of God's people have used over the course of time and place to continue telling their story.

The timeliness of the metaphors requires that stories must also be open-ended in order to allow the stories to evolve as the community grows and changes. However, this open-endedness creates discomfort. Theologically, metaphors are used to speak of God, yet no metaphor will ever perfectly or wholly capture God. Instead, we must often use multiple metaphors in tension and balance with one another. Even so, whether being used to speak theologically or ecclesiastically, no metaphor can ever claim to speak definitively for all time.[27] This supports not only McFague's argument regarding theological models but also what Brueggemann writes concerning the Hebrew community's conscious use of story: "The community was not concerned to communicate static meanings or flat memories to Israel's new generation. Rather, it was concerned about creating a context, evoking a perception, forming a frame of reference which went beyond and did not depend on . . . any particular narrative."[28] In other words, we communicate faith in stories because stories are faithful to the past while also flexible enough to be retold in the present voices and contemporary languages of the people.

A significant part of story's flexibility derives from the way in which it inspires the imaginations of its hearers. The Torah assumes an oral tradition in which the listener and speaker share near-equal parts. The sacred stories were interactive as they were told, inviting others into the drama and excitement. As oral communication gave way to the written word, the engagement of imagination took more intentionality.[29] Therefore, rabbinic traditions developed the practice of *midrash* for studying the Torah together, which sought to engage the story in and often behind and beneath the written texts. Hebrew scholar Wilda Gafney describes *midrash* as a sort of God wrestling in which readers ask questions of the text to which the text sometimes provides answers and sometimes does not. To answer the questions that the text will not, Gafney speaks of exercising the "sanctified imagination" by which the person enters the text in order to fill in the blanks—to tell "the story behind the story, the story between the lines on the page."[30]

Story invites listener and reader participation in a way that other forms of education and faith formation do not. And yet when we have lost the storiedness of the Bible, we no longer exercise our imaginations when reading it. We read Scripture for information rather than inspiration. When that happens, we are unmoved because we fail to encounter the stories and engage them the way they were intended to be heard. The stories no longer come alive in our minds, the words no longer evoke feelings, and the voice of God no longer seems to speak through them.

But God is still speaking.

We see, in the very existence of the Bible, evidence that the storying of faith is a canonical process necessarily taken up by every generation when confronted with new experiences or challenges to make sense of what is new in light of its history and tradition. The affirmation that "God is still speaking" serves as an invitation to churches and individual Christians to exercise their sanctified imaginations and see themselves as participating, through the storying of their faith experience, in that same confessional act as all God's people have done in every time and place. Each of our churches must access its collective imagination to see the story God is speaking and calling it into today. But before exploring what that story might be, I want to consider the spiritual posture of the storied faith.

Questions for Reflection

- What is your church's understanding of scriptural authority?
- How do you understand your church as participating in God's Story?
- What is the gospel in your particular time and place?

Like a Child

Whether conscious of it or not, every person, young or old, hears or reads the Bible and processes the sacred stories in relationship to their own life experiences. And yet within many of our churches, the only acceptable arenas for storied faith seem to be with either the very young (as in Christian education) or the very old (as in pastoral care). "For too long," laments Johann Baptist Metz, "we have tried to suppress the narrative potential of Christianity and have confined it to credulous children and old people."[31] We have been underutilizing a valuable asset to the church.

In Mark 10:15, Jesus says, "Truly I tell you, whoever does not receive the kingdom of God as a little child will never enter it" (NRSV). I believe Jesus says this in part because receiving God's kingdom occurs through a storied faith and thereby demands of would-be receivers an imagination most readily found in children. Jesus's words in Mark are suggestive that the storied faith must be reclaimed not only for children or the elderly but for people of all ages. This section will consider what might be learned from the way in which a child engages story and how this childlike approach may be a model for how churches engage the storied faith.

C. S. Lewis, writing at the intersection of Christian theology and children's literature, in addition to drawing from his own spiritual journey, reflected quite a bit about the function of story in the life of faith. He recognized the value of story not only for children but for adults as well, and he lamented the tendency for certain genres of literature to be relegated only to certain audiences. For instance, the idea that fairy tales belong only to children is a betrayal of the origin of most of those stories.[32] Instead, Lewis strove to write stories that could capture the imaginations of people of all ages, saying, "A children's story which is enjoyed only by children is a bad children's story."[33]

Fairy tales provoke a deeper yearning in the hearer or reader. Like the way that a myth captures a universal human experience through narrative, and a mundane story connects to some more sacred story, the fairy tale "stirs and troubles [a person] . . . with the dim sense of something beyond [their] reach and, far from dulling or emptying the actual world, gives it a new dimension of depth."[34] Rather than being absorbed and growing contented by the world around them, a person is invited through fairy tales to imagine there is something more meaningful to it. The above quotation concludes, "[One] does not despise real woods because [he or she] has read of enchanted woods: the reading makes all real woods a little enchanted." Stories, by ascribing to ordinary things imaginative or metaphorical significance, do a sacramental work and provoke us to wonder and awe.

See, for instance, the reverence with which a child will receive the bread and wine of the Eucharist. Although the child may not fully comprehend all of the theological underpinnings of the meal (do any of us, really?), having heard the story of Jesus sharing the Last Supper with his disciples, the child senses that there is something magical—something awesome—about it. This provocation of deeper yearning was part of a recent decision at PUCC to open its practice of communion to be inclusive of children in hopes that engaging them in the story and the partaking of the bread and wine would be part of stirring their spiritual longing. Unfortunately, this sort of decision is the opposite of what occurs in many congregations when they are faced with a choice between mystery and formality.

In many of our mainline churches, the stories with the power to provoke that spiritual longing have been reduced to templates for theological rigidity and legalism. We smother the mystical qualities of communion and baptism, incarnation and resurrection, beneath dogmatics and "doing it by the book." The results are often traditions and rituals that, having been stripped of the wonder and awe of story, are now devoid of their life-giving meaning. Churches offer story-less rituals and then complain about the younger generation's inattentiveness and unenthusiastic presence in worship. Alasdair MacIntyre warns, "Deprive children of stories and you leave them unscripted, anxious stutterers in their actions as in their words."[35] I don't think his warning is limited to children; adults suffer too when deprived of story. Our oftentimes stuttered, spastic, and stale worship and Christian witness are the evidence of a story-starved faith.

Not only do stories spark wonder; they also spark hope. Lewis and his contemporaries J. R. R. Tolkien and G. K. Chesterton each received criticism for the darker elements of their children's stories. Yet each defended their respective choices in a similar fashion by appealing to the ultimate outcome of those stories, insisting that fairy tales are stories of good news. Lewis argues adamantly that rather than shelter children from darkness, children ought to be shown darkness but also shown how goodness triumphs over it: "Since it is so likely that they will meet cruel enemies, let them at least have heard of brave knights and heroic courage. Otherwise, you are making their destiny not brighter but darker."[36] To ignore stories completely or to tell stories without any darkness does a disservice to the one tasked with living in a world fraught with both darkness and light. Instead, through stories, one might proclaim the ultimate victory of good over evil or, in more specific terms, the good news of God's victory through Jesus Christ. And in most instances, especially in today's story-centric world, encasing the good news in story is the most appropriate way to connect with your audience.[37]

In describing the Christian undertones of his *Chronicles of Narnia*, Lewis mused about the way in which a strict theological approach to Christianity can lead to a steely detachment from emotion. In other words, one might know the gospel in their head but not feel it in their heart. There might be a cognitive assent to terms and tenets but not the *pistis* belief described in Scripture. Moreover, apologetics fought on a battlefield of logic tend to result in angry stalemates or painful wounds. On the other hand, Lewis views story as an alternative vehicle for the truths of faith: "But supposing that by casting all these things into an imaginary world, stripping them of their stained-glass and Sunday school associations, one could make them for the first time appear in their real potency? Could one not thus steal past those watchful dragons? I thought one could."[38] Rather than starting with terms and tenets, begin with story.

In the case of children, story might be the most age-appropriate mode for communicating deep theological truths toward the development of a more mature faith. However, Lewis goes on to wonder whether the same strategy might not work for overcoming the obstacles in the minds of adults as well: "The inhibitions which I hoped my stories would overcome in a child's mind may exist in a grown-up's mind too, and may perhaps be overcome by the same means."[39] I believe Lewis's hunch is accurate—that story-centered faith development would indeed work at a multigenerational level and therefore that storytelling is not just a children's ministry. This is why our succumbing to the rationalist Nothing has had such an immobilizing effect.

In the church's attempts to be "enlightened"—to be serious and grown up—it has forsaken the storiedness of its faith. In putting away "childish" things, the church has set aside a crucial tool for learning to walk in darkness and combating evil. While not exactly a fairy tale like those Lewis told, Stephen King's classic novel It, which tells the story of a titular fiend tormenting a small Maine town, depicts this tension between growing up and the spiritual power of the imagination: "Can it be that It protects Itself by the simple fact that, as the children grow into adults they become either incapable of faith or crippled by a sort of spiritual and imaginative arthritis?"[40] In attempting to be reasonable and logical, Christians have lost our true religious language and our surest strength for warding off evil.

How can we articulate a storied faith in anything other than story? If the church is to recover the depth of truth and power to be found in God's promises, it must assume a childlike posture and receive anew its storied faith, and it must learn to speak that faith in forms that steal past the watchful dragons of our world. For the dragons to which C. S. Lewis alluded still exist as enemies to the storied faith—enemies both outside and within the church walls—determined to torch any notion of newness and change.

Questions for Reflection

- What place does story currently have in your church's ministry? With what age groups?

- What were some of your favorite childhood stories?

- What did those stories teach you?

Poetry, Prose, Prophets, and Parable

What if the "atrophy of narrative"[41] is not just a case of people trying to act grown up but also a result of our urge to control something that feels too flexible for comfort? What if churches opt for
programs, denominations for bullet-point statements of faith, and
individual Christians for bumper-sticker ethics because those
things are all more manageable than the inherent ambiguity of
theology by story? Then stories—"the original form of theological
expression"[42]—are either replaced with systematic treatises in the
name of order and orthodoxy or reclassified as timeless historical accounts rather than studied as subjective, creative products
of a particular place and time. Both paths result in the aforementioned loss of the storying imagination. It is, as Cone writes, "when
stories are abstracted from a concrete situation and codified into
Law or dogma that their life-blood is taken away and thus a people
begins to think that its ways of thinking and living are the only real
possibilities."[43]

Inasmuch as storytelling challenges this tendency toward
dogmatism and rigidity, it functions subversively. The storied faith
is a threat to the status quo because it allows for and assumes the
tenacity of newness and change, so those who enjoy and desire to
maintain privilege and power will often strive to silence the potentially subversive role of story. Without story and the imagination
it fosters in us, we cannot slay the guardian dragons. We remain
trapped in the status quo and the rigidity of "the way we've always
done it." Our faith, instead of being a dynamic celebration of a still-
speaking God who invites our participation in the liberation of the
oppressed and the making of all things new, becomes a static religion meant to comfort the affluent and oppressive.[44] Certainly, a
plausible argument could be made at this point, as I'm sure many
a liberation theologian would, that the absence of the storied faith
among predominantly white Christian traditions is far from coincidental but rather is a consequence of an intentional systemic effort
to absolutize and sanctify the white, straight, male, American Protestant lifestyle.

I agree.

Reducing stories to programs intentionally tempers them to make them safer and more conducive to maintaining the status quo. This is the strategy of every institutionally minded administration whose job it is to sustain the world as it is. Brueggemann observes this institutional mindset in the biblical kings: "Kings preside over and rely upon the consensus that this world is the one we have had and do have and will have. There is no other world except this one. . . . Kings embody and represent the endurance of the present, the eradication of a different past, and the prohibition of a different future."[45]

Stories, which long toward continuity—toward a bridge through the present between past and future—are poison to the kingly agenda. Therefore, kings will oppose stories in their effort to burn the bridges to past and future and isolate the present as the only time of consequence. In the words of Rage Against the Machine's powerful Orwellian cry, "Who controls the past now controls the future / Who controls the present now controls the past."[46] Kings want certainty and order, whereas stories threaten to bring questions and change. Because they lust for control, kings fear the movement stories encourage. In fact, kings will strive to censor any language of newness—namely, by silencing the voice of the prophets because prophets testify to a world of new possibilities.

The prophetic story, through its use of myth and metaphor, fosters in its hearers an imagination for a world different from the one at present. In his extensive writing on the prophets, Brueggemann contrasts the prosaic language of empire (i.e., the kings) with the poetic language of the prophets.[47] However, even nonprophetic writings in Scripture take on a prophetic function because of the story they tell. See, for instance, the story of Ruth as a check against the xenophobic reforms of Ezra and Nehemiah. See the story of Esther as a check against the hubris of royal (read also "patriarchal") governance.[48] Or see the story of Job as a check against the Deuteronomist's (and Job's friends') theology of cosmic karma. Jesus, too, often used stories to challenge the rigid ideologies of his audience. As opposed to the authoritative agenda the kings strive to maintain, the prophetic story serves as a "check against ideological thinking" because it refutes the dominant reality and proposes an alternative lens through which to understand life.[49]

One of the present critiques of Christianity in America is its seeming inability to separate itself from the idolatry of American nationalism. This is due, in part, to the fact that American Christians have gotten so used to speaking in the prose of empire that we have forgotten it is not our native tongue. The overlapping dialect between religion and country goes back at least as far as the founding fathers and the first Pilgrim settlers. After all, it was Congregationalist minister John Winthrop who famously asserted that the civilization founded in New England would become a "city on a hill" to the rest of the world. However, as time has passed, more and more of our poetic religious language has been reduced to national prose. Today, we have reached a point where the church often struggles to find the voice and vision to offer a meaningful, necessary critique of the nation.[50] To recover the storied faith is to recover the poetic and prophetic voice that dares to challenge the status quo and imagine other worlds in God's name.

Staying within the dichotomy that Brueggemann sets forth, the poetic, unlike the prosaic, allows space for tension because it does not rush to resolve pain or sadness or anger with theological platitudes, but rather it makes room for the full expression of grief and hurt as well as joy. The institutionally minded administration prefers prosaic platitudes over the poetry of story because it would rather perpetuate numbness than risk upsetting the status quo. So it is unsurprising that, in the absence of storied faith, mainline Christianity is regularly accused of having dull, emotionless spirituality. The renewal of storied faith aims to incorporate the whole range of human emotion. This renewal will not only impact the emotional health of the community but also help the church become a prophetic witness in refuting the world's aversion to dealing with suffering and death.[51] In addition to giving the church space for emotion, the poetry of story breaks through despair with a language of hope in God's promise of newness. Without that language, the church stays stuck. Or, as Brueggemann writes, "Where there is no tongue for new truth, we are consigned to the coldness of the old truth."[52] Stories give voice to the new truth.

However, as with Torah stories, prophetic stories are also localized to communities occupying particular times and places.[53] The prophetic story is determined by the social context, and when the present audience does not occupy the same or similar context, there can be a dissonance between the story being told and those hearing or reading it. This can make the prophetic stories of the Bible, which were predominantly written by oppressed minorities living under the rule of one totalitarian empire or another, difficult to teach and make accessible for mainline churches of predominantly white, middle-class suburbanites living in a free, democratic society. The stories of the prophets can oftentimes feel irrelevant to our experience. Walter Brueggemann goes so far as to muse whether the experience of some form of marginalization is a necessity for understanding the prophets properly: "Though it may be educationally difficult, an important implication is that the texts we regard as authoritative and canonical are in fact marginal in their origin and claims. Education may require experiencing that kind of marginality both in terms of social power and in terms of rationality."[54] I don't believe Brueggemann means to suggest mainline educators develop contrived experiences of marginalization. Rather, I believe his musing here reinforces just how critical it is for the mainline churches to listen to the voices and learn from the experiences of historically marginalized peoples.

Nevertheless, the prophetic task is not only to confront injustice and hypocrisy; it is also to provide the storied faith and storying imagination for speaking truth to power. When we attend to the prophetic insistence on using poetry and story, it convicts us of a common misconception we hold of prophets and the prophetic task: "In much of Protestantism, the prophets have been mistakenly understood as social activists or as social reformers. But they have the more fundamental task of nurturing poetic imagination."[55] Prophets are first and foremost storytellers. If the staid, prosaic church wants to recover its prophetic voice and task, it must begin by recovering its ability to think and speak in storied, poetic language. Thankfully, the church has a model in Jesus Christ because, as the late Rachel Held Evans rejoiced, "God With Us is a marvelous storyteller."[56]

Jesus lived in an oral culture and was almost exclusively an oral communicator. Throughout the Gospels, Jesus does a majority of his teaching and preaching in the form of stories called parables. Jesus scholar John Dominic Crossan defines *parable* as "a story deliberately calculated to show the limitations of myth, to shatter the world so that its relativity becomes apparent."[57] To Crossan's definition, I would add Sallie McFague's point that rather than "teach a spectator a lesson," a parable "invites and surprises a participant into an experience. This is its power, its power then and now to be revelatory, not once upon a time, but every time a person becomes caught up in it and by it."[58] Parables are intentionally subversive stories meant both to surprise and to change the hearer. Storytelling through parables is Jesus's preferred mode of prophetic protest and call to a transformed life. Jesus speaks in parables and performs parabolic actions to subvert the prevailing or dominant myths of the world and to reverse the expectations of his audience.[59] Jesus tells and embodies stories that humanize rather than dehumanize, free rather than oppress, heal rather than harm, and infuse the ordinary with a sacred meaning. One of the challenges for the church is to once again hear and read Jesus's parables as the prophetic stories they are.

Because what happens when the myth Jesus is subverting in Scripture is no longer a myth in our world? What happens when "our structure of expectation is not that of the original hearers of the parable," and it simply does not hit home?[60] Too frequently, when these questions have arisen, audiences have resolved the disconnect by turning Jesus's parables into moralistic fables or allegories because those were a more comfortable, accessible form.[61] Why? Because we instinctively resist change, and parables, due to their prophetic intent, provoke change more than any other story. We would rather go so far as to change the form of the story than let the story change us. However, parables require that we "let the story penetrate *us*, rather than look around for possible interpretations of it."[62] Christians and churches still make the mistake of moving Jesus's stories out of the realm of parables in order to avoid the call to change.

Parables threaten to shatter our world and make us vulnerable, yet it is in those moments that God and God's kingdom break through into our lives. If the church means to be renewed by God, it must dare to hear parables as the prophetic stories they are and not give in to the self-preserving instinct of the status quo. What might happen if a church dares to hear Jesus's parables as a subversion of its institutional myths? What if the trend of institutional decline is a parable in and of itself, one that the church has too long ignored or changed into some other kind of story in which we are still the heroes? What if we have errantly made the parables less about subverting the assumptions of our institutional world and more about determining what is wrong with everyone else?

A second challenge for the church is to talk about Jesus in terms of a storied faith. It is imperative that the church considers that the good news itself is presented in the Bible in storied form. In the years between his actual life and the accounts written *about* that life, faith in Jesus Christ became storied. The stories existed before any written Gospel did. Crossan's book, *The Power of Parable*, details the way that each Gospel writer is in effect telling a story about Jesus according to that writer's respective audience or agenda: "Jesus announced the Kingdom of God in parables, but the primitive church announced Jesus as the Christ, the Parable of God," and each Gospel writer applied and interpreted that parable in light of their particular language, geography, and culture.[63]

The best parable the church has to tell is the story of Jesus's life, death, and resurrection. Therefore, the church must tell it. Yet very often, sharing the faith through evangelism efforts is done in the institutionally minded forms of generalized bullet-point apologetics and doctrinal statements that fail to capture the localized storiedness of it all. In her memoir on the storiedness of Scripture, Rachel Held Evans marvels, "It strikes me as fruitless to try and turn the gospel into a statement when God so clearly gave us a story—or, more precisely, a person," and then suggests, in a way strikingly familiar to Brueggemann's comment about the Torah, "So when someone asks, 'What is the gospel?' the best response is, 'Let me tell you a story.'"[64]

Questions for Reflection

- How prophetic would you consider your church to be?

- How does your church react to prophetic voices of criticism?

- How frequently is your church exposed to stories of people whose experiences are radically different from your church's own?

Word Becomes Flesh Becomes Word Becomes Church

"In the beginning," the Gospel of John begins, echoing the elder's ancient origin story, "was the Word and the Word was with God and the Word was God. . . . Everything came into being through the Word, and without the Word nothing came into being" (John 1:1, 3 CEB). In the beginning was the Word—the *logos*, which is hard to define with any single English counterpart but might be best translated as "the Story" inasmuch as it refers to the ground of and reason for being. When that Word became flesh, God's Story became a human life, entering creation in order that all creation and human life might be redeemed to participate in that Story. As every quality filmmaker and storyteller knows, Jesus demonstrated that showing is more powerful than telling: "Jesus, as the parable of God, did not tell people *about* the kingdom but he *was* the kingdom; and the way his whole life brought people to the kingdom was through a juxtaposition of the ordinary within a startling new context."[65] Jesus exhibited the Story of God in the form of a human life's story. The incarnation, by which Word becomes flesh to bridge God and creation, is the ultimate bridge between mundane and sacred story.[66]

The story every Christian church has to tell is of Jesus Christ as a parable—*the* parable—in and for our particular place and time.

Story-centered renewal is about believing in Jesus as parable and about becoming a parabolic and prophetic church, in word and deed, telling and embodying a story that subverts the myths of the world today. For any church that is reclaiming its storied faith, the subsequent task is to discern its own word—its own particular story. What would it look like for a church to abide by McFague's insistence that "parabolic theology should be written as a story, not as a treatise"?[67] What would it look like for a church to proclaim its faith, identity, and mission, not in terms of mission statements but in terms of mission stories? Like the theological metaphors and stories communities have used for generations to speak about God, the metaphors and stories the church inevitably uses will be local, timely, and open-ended.[68] But more importantly, the story will be incarnated.

This chapter has emphasized the storiedness of the Christian faith, but the question that follows is, "How?" How do we practice the storied Christian faith? Narrative theology and practical theology both implore the embodiment of the storied faith: "The word which becomes flesh can become word for us again only through the flesh."[69] All the storied theology we can muster will not be enough on its own. The storied faith must be expressed in words *and* in deeds. For that reason, story-centered renewal involves not only theological discussions about the nature of God, the Bible, and the church but also conversations about local ministry and congregational life.

A Storied Community

Club or Community

"What's going to happen to us on Monday?"

It is a question that drives an iconic scene in John Hughes's classic *The Breakfast Club*, in which a diverse group of high school students has been sentenced to Saturday detention.[1] Up to this point in the film, the characters have discovered only one commonality among them: a shared dislike for their principal. However, as they gather in a circle at the back of the library, Brian asks the above question, interested in knowing whether that single commonality is enough to establish community—to make them friends beyond the boundaries of that Saturday morning.

The conversation that follows is one full of honesty, anger, vulnerability, and laughter as characters confess true feelings, confront one another's shortcomings, and share stories of how they ended up serving their Saturday sentence. The scene is famous for the raw emotion it captures, making it feel like a holy moment within the film. In fact, it is a transformative moment because from that point, the group of teens recognizes that despite facing different circumstances and being part of different social cliques, they share many of the same struggles and pressures that come with the experiences of being a teenager. This scene is where the breakfast *club* becomes a *community*.

"What's going to happen to us on Monday?" could also be asked in churches, especially those in the Protestant mainline who have often been criticized as acting more like country clubs than communities of faith. In those churches where attending Sunday morning worship seems to be the only thing its people hold in common, it is fair to wonder whether the space we occupy and relationships we have on Sunday mornings are circumstantial rather than sacred. The difference between club and community is story. Storytelling, which requires both honesty and vulnerability, is, as *The Breakfast Club* illustrates, key to the formation of authentic Christian community.

In chapter 2, I emphasized story as a central theological mode of the Christian faith. The counterpart to a storied faith is the storied community formed around that faith. In this chapter, I will emphasize story as a central organizing practice of the church. Whereas chapter 2 approached story-centered renewal through a biblical/theological lens, this chapter will approach story-centered renewal through an ecclesial/praxeological lens. The key questions to be explored are, "Why is a storied community the best vehicle for a storied faith? Aside from the purpose of faith formation, what are the fruit born by a storytelling church? Moreover, how would bearing those fruit help meet the existential needs of the church and the world around it?"

To begin answering those questions, I will reiterate the assertion of chapter 1 that isolationism is having a severely negative impact on the social fabric of local mainline churches and their communities. Most interpersonal connectivity is limited or superficial in nature. However, I believe with Dietrich Bonhoeffer that "Christian brotherhood [read: fellowship] is not an ideal which we must realize; it is rather a reality created by God in Christ in which we may participate."[2] In their current state of isolation, our communities are missing out on sharing in a gift of God.

Stories are the foremost tool for creating this sort of sacred space for authentic connection and Christian fellowship. Stories foster honesty, vulnerability, and forgiving relationships in a way that bylaws and doctrinal statements cannot. A church constitution may dictate rules and processes for decision-making, but it does not guarantee that a congregation will navigate change and conflict in a healthy, relational manner. A church credo may dictate the communal theology, but it does not guarantee the flexibility or the room necessary for spiritual growth. On the other hand, the culture of any particular church—the atmosphere of the community itself—exists through its stories. Stories are more incarnational than doctrine. Stories are the way that a church culture is shaped and transmitted to new members and the next generation. Just as faith is best communicated through story, so too the culture and tradition of the community are best communicated through its stories.[3] Stories are the glue that holds individuals together in community, binding us to one another. A crucial tenet of narrative theology is the imperative that the community be shaped by a storied faith. Without that narrative—without that story—the bond of the community and its power to draw others into faith weakens.

Years ago, I read a book by Canadian pastor Bruxy Cavey. One particular line from the book continues to influence my conception of church and ministry: "Truly, there is no holier ground than the space between you and me as we connect in honest, vulnerable, forgiving relationship."[4] For the church to be renewed, it must rediscover the storiedness of its community and re-create that sacred, holy space between its members. It must undertake the difficult but necessary work of inviting people to share their stories. The re-creation of that holy space in which stories are shared of God's work and presence in peoples' lives is essential to deepening relationships and fostering healthy dynamics, especially in the midst of change.

Within every congregation, but especially within a changing or struggling church, oppositional camps and/or a diversity of opinions may arise around particular issues or decisions. A storied community is equipped with the tools to handle disagreement. Conflict resolution experts value the practice of storytelling in large part for the leveling effect it has in diverse or oppositional group settings and its ability to build bridges of empathy across ideological divisions. Storytelling space is sacred because it affirms the equal value of each person's voice by insisting that each one's story deserves to be told and heard. Conflict mediation specialist Tom Porter writes, "We each need to tell our story, and we each need to hear the other's story. Being listened to provides the opening we need to tell our stories, to express feelings and ideas we would otherwise be afraid to voice."[5] Especially in the midst of struggle and difficult decisions, storytelling is a collaborative alternative to what can become an adversarial enterprise. When the changes involved in church renewal create tension, that tension is best managed and mediated through story because storytelling has the power to transform perspectives and relationships.[6]

Fellow conflict mediators Kenneth Cloke and Joan Goldsmith define conflict resolution work itself as the "successful creation of a composite story." The end result of telling and listening to each other's stories and unpacking them for deeper truths is the formation of a unified story that doesn't necessarily represent agreement but rather a commitment to moving forward together—"a story of how they overcame their difficulties and worked together to create a common story."[7] Stories offer an avenue for understanding and reconciliation, both of which are imperative in congregational renewal. More importantly, the creation of a unified story that brings the community together in spite of personal differences may become that binding story that shapes congregational culture for generations to come.

Yet as valuable as story is, it is also a demanding practice that requires a great deal from its participants. Porter writes, "Telling our own story is not easy, because it demands self-revelation, vulnerability, and self-knowledge."[8] Many church members are unprepared to meet those demands, and many communities are unable to equip them. Self-revelation, vulnerability, and self-knowledge require an established attitude of introspection, honesty, and trust that many churches simply have not worked to develop. Becoming a storied community means more than instituting the practice of storytelling and expecting that people will immediately open up and bare their souls to one another; it means creating that holy ground between people in an environment where stories can be safely told. As such, before suggesting what would be the characteristics of a storied Christian community, I will lift up an example of a storied community that has effectively incorporated story as a central practice by creating this sacred and safe environment.

Questions for Reflection

- In your faith community, how much fellowship is there between church members beyond worship gatherings?

- What conflicts do you see emerging in conversations about church renewal and change?

- What opportunities are there for sharing and listening to each other's concerns?

Stories in Alcoholics Anonymous

Alcoholics Anonymous (AA) is an example of what a storied community might look like and the fruit it could bear. Twelve-step recovery programs, while not identifying with any specific religion, borrow heavily from religious language.[9] Nevertheless, because of their intentional noncommittal to any particular creed, AA and other twelve-step recovery programs are frequently written off as too secular or nonsectarian to have a place in an ecclesial conversation.[10] However, I highlight them here because they function on several levels as the quintessential storied community.

In studying the storiedness of AA groups, Keith Humphreys argues, "If one views AA as a spiritually-based community rather than solely as a clinical intervention, one will quickly observe that AA is brimming with stories."[11] He goes on to note that most of the Big Book—the sacred text of the AA community—is a compilation of members' stories and that most meetings are spent telling and hearing stories of those in recovery. AA and other twelve-step programs are guided by the core story of recovery and gathered around the ongoing telling of that story through the lives of their members. Like the way in which storied faith is carried from past into the future by being told presently, "the AA community narrative is composed primarily of past members' personal stories, but also shapes the current personal stories of newer members."[12] By considering the ways in which these organizations centralize story and the characteristics it evokes in those communities and the lives of their members, the church may learn how story-centered renewal strengthens the community itself.

While the Twelve Steps are more widely known and share many theological parallels with Christian teaching, the Twelve Traditions— the suggested organizational guidelines of AA groups—are what hold them together as story-centered communities.[13] The Twelve Traditions were forged by the trials of early AA groups as they encountered questions and obstacles to community life. Out of these experiences, Alcoholics Anonymous derived an organizational philosophy for sustaining the community itself. If the goal of the Twelve Steps is the health of individuals within AA, then the goal of the Twelve Traditions is the vitality of the AA community.

The main emphasis throughout the Twelve Traditions is on maintaining the presence of personal autonomy without its costing communal unity. The traditions articulate a tension that will be familiar to many local congregations, particularly in the UCC. Whether regarding the relationship of the local congregation to its middle judicatory or the national church, or in the relationship of individual members to the church itself, the balance of autonomy and communal authority is constantly being weighed. The Twelve Traditions hone in on that tension and offer wisdom for maintaining the health of the institution both locally and more broadly, because in the view of AA's founders, "the group must survive or the individual will not."[14] In other words, because the community is made up of broken members, the community itself must function wholly. Though it goes largely unwritten in the traditions themselves, the leveling power of story permeates the AA understanding that each individual offers a unique voice to the group, and yet no one person is more important than the rest.[15] Each person's story is valuable, but no one's story supersedes the story of recovery. The Twelve Traditions strike a covenantal balance between inclusivity and purity of story that enables AA communities to thrive and grow.

The first quality that makes AA a quintessential storied community is its radically inclusive perspective on membership. Tradition Three declares that the sole requisite for membership is the desire to quit drinking: "No matter who you are, no matter how low you've gone, no matter how grave your emotional complications—even your crimes—we still can't deny you AA. We don't want to keep you out."[16] (It is fascinating hearing the echoes of this tradition in the UCC mantra, "No matter who you are or where you are on life's journey, you are welcome here.") The only requirement for being part of the AA community is the desire to join oneself to the story of recovery.

A second distinctive quality of AA is its corporate commitment to telling a singular story. The group's sole organizational purpose is to carry the story of recovery to others who need it.[17] Recovery is its *only* story. The organization is so explicitly focused on recovery that several of the traditions instruct against involving the group or the "Alcoholics Anonymous" name in external issues or controversies in order to avoid misconstruing the core story and muddying the healing waters.[18] But also the centralization of a core story stems from a belief that the organization is most successful in achieving its mission when its energies are not split across multiple goals.

Inclusivity and singularity of story are how Alcoholics Anonymous maintains its institutional vitality. AA does not grow through mass advertising or clever marketing schemes. Rather, it grows as the stories of its members and their transformed lives attract other people in search of that same transformative story for their own lives.[19] By sustaining the health of the community, the Twelve Traditions allow for the ongoing, life-giving practice of storytelling to foster the journey of recovery.

In his analysis of AA and its stories, George H. Jensen surmises, "Its culture and rituals frame and support a unique approach to storytelling."[20] Therefore, I will now turn to the particular forms the story of recovery takes within the community gatherings of AA. By understanding the unique storytelling practices and the way in which different kinds of stories serve varying functions within an AA group, I will suggest parallel functions stories may have in the life of the church.

The most familiar genre of AA story is the "drunk-a-log," which begins "Hi, I'm an alcoholic . . ." and then tends to have three distinct parts: who the person was in their drinking state, what happened to begin the path of recovery, and who the person is now as a result of AA.[21] In the church, we might call the drunk-a-log a "testimony," and in chapter 5, I will look more closely at the practice and place of testimony in the story-centered church. In AA, however, the drunk-a-log serves multiple purposes benefiting both the listeners and the speaker. Humphreys points out that to the speaker, "composing and sharing one's drunk-a-log is a form of self-teaching. . . . Members learn to construct their drunk-a-logs in such a way that they parallel AA philosophy about alcoholism."[22] The drunk-a-log exercises those demands of self-revelation, vulnerability, and self-knowledge. Eventually, this process of story-making and telling sync the individual's story to the communal AA story. Moreover, Humphreys argues, "By turning their past into a story (i.e., a drunk-a-log), alcoholics gain power and reflexivity over their alcoholic experiences. The experiences of the old self are thus reinterpreted in the new self's frame, bringing those experiences into AA's interpretive ambit."[23] In other words, by integrating one's personal story into the community's core story, the pathway is opened for transformation to occur as the story of recovery works into the person's life.

Drunk-a-logs are monologic in that they are told to "listeners who only listen." However, Jensen notes, "AA stories are certainly dialogic in the broader sense that one speaker's story is followed by another's. Each person learns not just from the telling but also from how his or her story positions itself within the context of other people's stories."[24] In telling the drunk-a-log, the teller sees how their story is simultaneously unique and yet connected to the communal story. In telling their story, the teller becomes more deeply engrained in the community, its tradition, and its values.[25] But also listeners recognize in the teller's story familiar elements from their own stories. Like testimonies in the church, drunk-a-logs are not only formational for the teller but also evangelical to the listeners.[26]

A second genre of story in Alcoholics Anonymous is serial stories, which are more interactive than drunk-a-logs and often occur at meetings focused on a specific theme or step. Humphreys states, "Once the focus is determined, each member gives a brief account of his or her experience with the topic. Speakers often agree with or elaborate on the accounts of previous speakers, thus building a community narrative on the meaning of the topic for AA members."[27] Like the living tradition of a storied faith, serials suggest an open and ongoing conversation with past experiences and current circumstances to discern how recovery is achieved and sustained today. Like the notion of continuing testament, mentioned in chapter 2, the "communal and open hermeneutic [of AA] continually renews its texts" through serial stories.[28] Still, inasmuch as preachers may try to address contemporary issues in light of scriptural wisdom, traditional sermons delivered by a pastor from the pulpit tend to lack the multivocal character of serial stories in AA. Within congregational life, serial stories can be most closely likened to a topical small group study in which leadership is shared among participants and the conversation centers around a specific subject.

A third genre of story in AA is the apologue, which is "a narrative that gives an explanation for why a particular procedure or tradition is present in the AA community."[29] For example, why does Tradition Ten suggest groups not get involved in outside issues? There is an apologue about an early AA group that angrily split following a dispute over whether to publicly pledge support for a political candidate supporting strong temperance laws. Apologues link the present to the experiences of the past but with the hope of grounding practices and traditions in the community's core story and avoiding the repetition of prior mistakes. In churches, there are traditions and practices to which some members may know the apologue but that other members see as unconnected and irrelevant to the congregation's story. For instance, if one knows the story of when the pastor tripped down the chancel steps carrying the Christ candle out of the Good Friday Tenebrae service in the pitch-black sanctuary, then leaving the altar lights lit does not seem so sacrilegious. Through apologue, the experiences of the past and the lessons learned get woven into the fabric of the communal story.

Legends function similarly to apologues in that they offer wisdom in the present from the experiences of the past. Legends, however, are more personal in scope than apologues. Legends illustrate the way in which "some individuals' personal stories are adopted into the community narrative, which in turn shapes the personal stories of future members."[30] In every local church, there are legends told of forebears in faith, their spiritual journeys, and their lasting contributions to the community. These legends are not only reminders of the church's collective memory but also assurances that as each of us shares our stories and our lives with the community, they become part of that same collective memory.

The final genre of story told in AA and other twelve-step groups are humorous stories. These self-deprecating stories are essential to the AA community because "humorous stories allow AA members to acknowledge their foibles in a non-threatening way while maintaining the humility which is considered critical to recovery."[31] Laughter is a catalyst for humility and connection that cannot occur when shame and the defenses of keeping up appearances are at work. Jensen suggests, "In a room where people are laughing one moment and crying the next, there is less pressure to 'bullshit' others. It is carnival that makes communion possible."[32] The ability to laugh at ourselves—and more importantly, to laugh together—makes it more likely that we can accept one another. Richard Rohr may argue that "deep communion and dear compassion is formed much more by shared pain than by shared pleasure," but the enduring importance of humorous stories indicates that shared pleasure cannot be done without.[33]

Indeed, none of the five types of story in AA can be omitted if the storied community is to function in a healthy manner. As such, the story-centered church would do well to integrate each type of story into its own congregational life. The practice and presence of these five types of story in AA result in two distinct communal qualities that are crucial qualities to be had in Christian churches: an attitude of confession and a commitment to covenantal fellowship.

In the following section, I will argue that confession and fellowship are often lacking in the church despite being desperately needed in today's spiritual climate and that they are qualities that can be sparked and strengthened through the practice of story. Inasmuch as its storiedness helps foster these qualities, AA and other twelve-step groups have much wisdom to offer the local church.

Questions for Reflection

- What is your church's familiarity with AA or other recovery programs?
- Which, if any, of the five types of story are already regularly practiced in your church?
- Which of the five types of story seem easiest to implement? Most difficult?

Confession in Community

In *Life Together*, his landmark meditation on Christian community, Dietrich Bonhoeffer posits that one of the fundamentals of authentically "Christian" community is confession. He famously laments over churches so concerned with the appearance of piety that members are unable to acknowledge their sinfulness: "The pious fellowship permits no one to be a sinner. So everybody must conceal his sin from himself and from the fellowship. We dare not be sinners. Many Christians are unthinkably horrified when a real sinner is suddenly discovered among the righteous. So we remain alone with our sin, living in lies and hypocrisy. The fact is that we are sinners!"[34] Bonhoeffer suggests confession as the antidote to falsity and isolation. Confession breaks through seclusion, pride, and shame and in their place builds empathy, humility, and grace.

Breaking through pride and stubbornness in order to build humility and transformation is the primary aim of the Twelve Steps and the storytelling practices of AA. In Step Four, AA members are invited to take a "fearless moral inventory" of themselves.[35] Step

Five involves "admitting to God, to ourselves, and to another human being the exact nature of our wrongs" and is but the first of a series of steps through which individuals make efforts toward atonement and reconciliation.[36] It is difficult not to see the common reverence with which both Bonhoeffer and twelve-step programs view the practice of confession. Bonhoeffer writes, "In the presence of a psychiatrist I can only be a sick man; in the presence of a Christian brother I can dare to be a sinner."[37] The founders of Alcoholics Anonymous likewise view Step Five as freedom from isolation: "Until we had talked with complete candor of our conflicts, and had listened to someone else do the same thing, we still didn't belong. Step Five was the answer. It was the beginning of true kinship with man and God."[38] Because it proposes that in the grace and acceptance of another person, we see reflected the grace and acceptance of God, it is not unreasonable to call the confession described in Step Five "sacramental."[39] As practiced in AA and depicted in the aforementioned scene from *The Breakfast Club*, confession is an integral part of fostering holy space between people.

That initial moment of confession in Step Five is the beginning, but ongoing confessional storytelling is the primary mode by which individuals practice the steps of recovery.[40] In the AA practice of telling humorous and drunk-a-log stories, the two most confessional of the five types, the masks that would hide our brokenness are removed. Likewise, in the confessional attitudes and practices of a storied community, sinners do not have to conceal themselves from the whole. Like the alcoholic who admits "I'm an alcoholic" to a group of fellow alcoholics or the pressure-laden jock who acknowledges that his display of toxic masculinity was merely an attempt to hide his insecurity, the sinner who confesses to being a sinner moves "from denying what they are and feeling alienated from others, even from themselves and their own bodies, to accepting what they have been and what they will always be even as they begin to feel like members of a new community."[41] Furthermore, Jensen quotes an AA member who attended meetings as a way of remembering that he is not alone in the struggle for recovery.[42] I suggest that worship gatherings and fellowship might function that way for the members of storied church communities as reminders that we are not alone in the struggle against sin.

For instance, while it would certainly prolong proceedings a bit, what if Sunday morning worship began each week with each respective congregant, one by one, rising, stating their name, and saying, "Hi, I'm a sinner," then proceeding to tell a brief story of some misdeed or missed opportunity from the previous week, the sense of conviction, and the assurance of God's grace? What would that congregation be like? For as far-fetched and uncomfortable as such an idea may sound, maybe that in itself is telling of how stoic and secretive our churches have become. Presumably, a community with such a confessional practice would be free from the inhibitions of self-righteousness that Bonhoeffer saw stifling authenticity in many churches. Just as the confessional stories of AA connect members to one another, the practice of *corporate* storied confession in the church would foster humility and transformation in individuals as well as a communal identity and bond.

I stress "corporate" above because Bonhoeffer identifies two potential pitfalls of placing such emphasis upon confession. The first is the notion that a solitary person should be the confessor for all others. Bonhoeffer is wary of the burden and power that would stem from a singular person hearing all confessions. Instead, a corporate confession like that practiced in AA consists of all members making and hearing confessions. This way, even hearing confession becomes a participatory act: "The audience participates in the speaker's confession as if it were their own."[43] As if confirming Bonhoeffer's fear, Richard Rohr laments the way in which Christian communities have neglected the corporate nature of confession and made it an individualized, privatized practice. "What was lost," he writes, "was a healing and forgiving community." Unlike Step Five practices in AA, privatized confession "did not create strong peer relationships in the community or the family."[44] Indeed, even the way many congregations have practiced "corporate" confession has undermined its potential effect. In Sunday morning liturgy, a corporate confession is often a generalized unison prayer read aloud by the congregants without a guarantee of transformative resonance or the goal of communal bonding over shared pain or experience. Instead of contributing to the formation of a holy space between members, confession (even that called "corporate") has been used to reinforce their sense of isolation. The storied community must reverse that trend by ensuring that confession occurs within the context of trusting fellowship.

It should go without saying that not everyone in the church will be comfortable with the confessional component of the storied community.[45] The founders of AA encountered that same dilemma and describe several types of people who may respond poorly to the self-critical aspects of confession: the "depressive" will be so overwhelmed by the extent of sin that they will reach a point of resigned hopelessness not unlike Kierkegaard's sickness unto death, the "self-righteous" will compose a superficial list of easily band-aided sins but never approach the root of the problem, and the "avoidant" will resist taking personal responsibility for their sins and instead shift the blame to someone or something else.[46] Each of these people is sure to show up in our churches too, but their presence should not prohibit our becoming a storied community.

The other danger that Bonhoeffer warns against is turning confession—or in this case, confessional storytelling—into an end in itself. It is always a means to an end. In AA, sharing one's story is a part of working out the steps and working the path to recovery. The story of recovery, like the story of redemption, is continuously being worked out in the lives of those who claim it. Step Ten of the twelve-step program suggests taking a continued personal inventory, even beyond the initial confession, which never stops looking at assets and liabilities with the humble admission that "we shall look for progress, not for perfection."[47]

The twelfth of the Twelve Steps stresses the importance of sharing the message of recovery with other alcoholics, which means acknowledging the change and transformation one has undergone out of a desire to spark the hope of change in someone else. Confession and storytelling are both ultimately about speaking change into being, which is why Bonhoeffer warns that, in the Christian community, confession cannot be allowed to become a routine of works righteousness. Rather, it must be a means toward humility and transformed lives.[48] Confession is about acknowledging a change that has already occurred and change that will continue to occur. The same is true of storytelling. For that reason, the storied community is about more than just its people telling their stories; it is about its people living out God's Story together.

Questions for Reflection

- How is confession practiced in your church?
- How is sin spoken or not spoken of in contexts of worship and fellowship?
- What place do you understand confession having in the story of redemption?

Transformed and Transforming

One of the challenges to characterizing the gospel as a storied faith is the critique that calling it "story" undermines its claim to truth. But as John Navone points out, the storied community, in essence, proves the storied faith: "The truth of the Gospel story is witnessed by saints that have been formed by its narrative power for producing truthful lives. The truthfulness of our lives is the existential verification of the claims of the Gospel story; it is the evidence that the story has been heard properly, and that it is true."[49]

While one could argue that the decline of churches across American Christianity is due to a secularization of society and increased skepticism toward any claim to truth, I would argue that the blame falls more heavily on churches who have failed to be living proof of the story they espouse, in large part because they have failed to understand it is a story they're telling. This is why congregational renewal should focus on the congregation recovering its storiedness: "Our grasp of the Gospel story is determined by the story that our life tells."[50] The storied Christian community, by its practicing life, tells the story of lives transformed by Jesus and of a world still being transformed through him.

Redemption is a story of good news best proclaimed by those who have been redeemed. Transformation is a hope best spoken by those who have been transformed. However, this means that for our churches, storytelling must become more than an occasional practice of the community; it must become the transforming way of a community transformed by Christ. As Leonard Sweet argues, "The church needs to become a culture of storytellers," because "if it takes a thousand voices to tell a single story, it takes all our voices to tell the Jesus story."[51] The storied faith requires a storied community as its vehicle. Just as the witness of transformed lives is the only advertising Alcoholics Anonymous needs, the church can be (and should be) Christianity's best source of marketing.

In the following chapter, I will further explore the idea of story-centered marketing by surveying how it has been utilized in the arenas of business and communications. If the mainline church is going to proclaim and embody a transformative story, what might it learn from experts in these fields about crafting and conveying that story in order to tell a true and faithful story in a world of fabrication?

Finding a Story amid the Stories

You Already Have a Story

"Go then. There are other worlds than these."[1] With those ominous words, Jake Chambers grants the Gunslinger permission to let go.

As suggested in chapter 1, many mainline congregations need to let go of whatever has been their core congregational story. Letting go can be painful, but there is a balm in those words Jake utters to Roland of Gilead: we need not remain captive. If stories have the power to create worlds, then there will, indeed, be another world created when the church learns to tell and inhabit another story. However, the church must find its next story with care, because not all stories are equally beneficial in the short and long term. Not all the new worlds we can create are good for the future health of the congregation.

People today are surrounded and bombarded by stories, many of which send conflicting messages about truth and the world. Some stories are imbued with optimism, bending toward peace, justice, and/or happiness. Others follow a less hopeful arc toward doom, judgment, and/or death. Some stories inspire hope; others, fear. In its underlying arc, every possible story bears the potential for different lasting consequences—having the ability to shape life for the better or the worse. For instance, Annette Simmons notes the short-term allure of fear stories over those of hope: "Since fear is easier to activate than hope, people see a fear story work first, and stick with it."[2] The tragic story inspires fear. Many churches today have amassed and continue to sustain significant membership numbers based on a story of fear—the story of a secular world set against the will of God, hell-bent on persecuting the faithful. Simmons goes on to caution, "Inevitably, the churches that preach fear stories are the very ones that suffer from infighting, hypocrisy, back-biting, and gossip. The churches that preach hope stories better nurture community and compassion and become places where everyone feels welcome."[3] While hope stories may not produce the same short-term gains as fear stories, they are more beneficial to the long-term health of the congregation.

Psychologist Dan McAdams warns that although a story can relieve existential dread, there are circumstances in which it may not provide relief. He asserts, "Many of the same problems that plague badly told stories can be discerned in narratives of human identity. In the context of personal myth, underdeveloped characters, inopportune images, childish themes, or stalled plots are not mere aesthetic concerns—they result in real human malaise."[4] Given McAdams's assertion about the plague of the bad story, choosing the wrong new story may compound the existential crisis for an already dying church and, instead of renewing it, could serve as the final nail in the coffin.

However, one of the underlying fears of struggling churches is the belief that the window for saving themselves has already passed and that they must seek outside help. They feel pressured to select a new story from the story-saturated world around them. When the church has lost the storiedness of its faith and succumbed to the belief that its new story exists in the vague somewhere out there, it either quickly grows overwhelmed by the sheer abundance of stories from which it has to choose, grasps haphazardly at every story that crosses its path, or remains paralyzed with fear, uncertain how to find its new story. Story-centered renewal rejects each of those options. Annette Simmons acknowledges, "Most storytelling advice has you constructing a story from the outside in," in which the first concerns are the wants and expectations of the audience.[5] However, both she and prolific storyteller Stephen King recommend a different approach to story construction based on the belief that finding a story is better achieved by first looking inward rather than outward.

Throughout his memoir on the craft of writing, King describes his story-development process not as groping in the dark for a bright idea and waiting for an epiphany but rather like carefully excavating a fossil from the dirt.[6] The faintest glimpse of a possible story inspires the delicate and deliberate work of mining the whole of it out from where it is buried. It is at once a work of risk and care. But also it is an affirmation of one's creative self. The story is already there. You have everything you need. You just need to draw the story out for it to be usable.

Story-centered renewal declares that the church already possesses the story it needs in the storied faith of a storied community. It simply must be brought to the surface. The church story may lie buried beneath generations of dirt swept under the rug and dust brushed off the hymnals, but it can be excavated with the same balance of risk and care in what, for the church, is a process of discernment. I use the word *discernment* because it suggests a prayer-laden decision-making process. Discernment connotes the persistence and precision of the careful fossil-hunting archaeologist. The church must go about finding its new story with patience, wisdom, and the leading of the Holy Spirit. But more importantly, discernment suggests that the church need not scour the worldly marketplace of stories. Rather, it need only look within to find its story and then work diligently and delicately to bring that story out.

Story-centered renewal may still be relatively untested in ecclesial settings, but it is already well established in the worlds of marketing and business. The insights gleaned from the way in which those arenas have harnessed the power of story will help inform the proposed ways that story can (and cannot) function in church renewal. There are four authors, in particular, who recognize that the role of storytelling in various fields can be useful in applying story-centered thinking to the church.

First, I have already mentioned Annette Simmons, who is a lecturer on storytelling and has written two books, *The Story*

Factor (2006) and *Whoever Tells the Best Story Wins* (2015), based on her experiences teaching storytelling for business and organizational purposes. She also affirms storied thinking as having immense institutional value to the church. Next, Seth Godin's 2009 book *All Marketers Are Liars* focuses primarily on the use of story in branding and selling products because of the ability of narrative to connect with consumers and shape the public perception of the company. However, he is cognizant of the way in which churches in the twenty-first century must market themselves. Third, Stephen Denning's *The Leader's Guide to Storytelling* (2011) lives up to its lofty title. Denning is a globally recognized consultant on narrative for leadership and business. As he traces the role of story in the organization and the way story is utilized by leaders within those organizations, there are many insights that parallel not only story's place in the church but also the way that story is wielded by pastors and lay leaders. Last, Christian Salmon's book *Storytelling: Bewitching the Modern Mind* (2017) is a profound overview of contemporary storytelling. In addition to covering the impact of story on marketing and organization, he delves into the political manipulation of narrative. Throughout the book, he uses religious language to suggest that faith and/or belief are also influenced by the power of the story. In applying storied thinking to church renewal, I am indebted to the wisdom and warnings offered by each of these authors in their respective works.

The purpose of this chapter is to build upon the enduring hopefulness of the storied faith discussed in chapter 2, the transformative potential of the storied community discussed in chapter 3, and the insights of storied thinkers in the arenas of business, marketing, and communication in order to begin crafting a new church story that offers long-term benefit to the congregation. Moreover, the goal of this chapter is to establish the discernment process of a church story as an ongoing, cyclical practice of the community. To do so, I will be giving storied language to a practical theological framework for self-reflection originally put forth by Thomas Groome.

Groome titles the process "shared praxis" because it is intended to be "a group of Christians sharing in dialogue their critical reflection on present action in light of the Christian Story and its Vision toward the end of lived Christian faith."[7] Groome's shared praxis approach (see figure 4.1) involves five steps composing the full critical reflection a faith community undergoes as it discerns and gives life to its story. However, it is crucial to my usage of Groome's framework to note that while he lists its steps sequentially, in the process of critical reflection, they can and often do happen concurrently.

The first step is the *observation*. Here, the congregation describes and assesses its current practices. The church looks at itself and its present practices and asks, "What are we doing? What is the story we are already telling?" This step may entail something like an inspection of church literature (brochures, newsletters,

FIGURE 4.1. Groome's shared praxis cycle

website, etc.), the building, the worship experience, or current programs.

The second step is the *critical reflection* upon those practices in their present enactment, tracing how those practices came into community life, and how those practices might look in the future. In other words, the church asks, "*Why* are we doing them?" and "Where did they come from?" Here, knowledge of the church's origin story and some of its sacred and apologue stories will be helpful.

The third step is group *dialogue*, during which people talk and listen to one another about how the current practices are meaningful (or not) to them. This step tests the resonance of the communal story with the individual stories of its members. As noted earlier, conflict may arise if people have different opinions of the meaningfulness of current practices, but it is still essential to give voice in the dialogue to all perspectives.

The fourth step is when the church asks whether the current practices are representative of who the community is and what it believes. This step involves bringing the current practices into conversation with the storied faith—the normative Scriptures and traditions of the community—what Groome calls the *Story*. For Groome, the *Story* encompasses "the whole faith tradition of our people however that is expressed or embodied."[8] Groome's definition is crucial to this part of the approach because it does not relegate the Story only to sacred Scriptures but rather presumes that the Story is unfinished. Even as the church holds the Bible and Christian tradition up somewhat objectively in order to reflect critically on its practices, we are simultaneously a part of writing the next chapter. The Story is still ours. Groome insists, "We must appropriate the Story critically within the present experience, reclaim it, add to it with our own creative word, and in that sense 'change' it."[9]

The fifth step in Groome's methodology is to consider, in light of the community's story and the Story, whether the current practices are appropriate, and if they are not, to consider what *new practices* might be more appropriate and to implement those practices. Here, the church asks and answers, "Is there something else we should be doing? Is there another story to tell?"

Then the cycle begins again.

That is the important part. Like the shared praxis approach, story-centered church renewal isn't a one-time fix from struggle to new life. It is an entryway into a continuous cycle of communal reflection and change that ensures the church's story is always "ours" to the people of that time and place. The practical theological work of a story-centered community is to be consistently engaged in a critically reflective analysis of its practices through the rubric of its story and God's Story.

At the risk of oversimplifying, I suggest that the story-centered community tends to handle story and hold it in three simultaneous ways. Christian educator Julie Anne Lytle labels this trinity as story-keeping, storytelling, and story-making: "As story-keepers, community members maintain the wisdom of their tradition and orient the community toward [God's vision]. As storytellers, community members share this vision of life with God and invite others into their understanding of it. As story-makers, community members move from faith to action, putting their beliefs into practice, and adding their witness to the Christian Story."[10] Using Lytle's trio of labels, I will explore the essential qualities of a healthy church story: particularity, authenticity, and congruency. At the end of the day, the church is free to choose its new story. But choosing the right story matters. It must be a healthy story if it is to both garner immediate enthusiasm and hold long-term benefit to the congregation. The wrong story will be poorly received by large portions of the congregation or short lived in its impact. In order for the church's new story to be healthy, it must possess those three essential qualities, each of which juxtaposes a temptation facing churches searching for a story amid a world bombarded by stories. The story the church keeps must be particular rather than generic. The story it tells must be authentic rather than imitative. And the story it makes must be congruent rather than manipulative. Each subsequent section will address one of those qualities in further detail.

Questions for Reflection

- Would you say your church is more easily motivated by fear or by hope? Why?

- What influence, if any, do business/marketing trends currently have upon your church?

- How does the fourth step of Groome's shared praxis cycle (Story) assume the storiedness of faith as discussed in chapter 2?

Keeping a Particular (Not Generic) Story

Story-keeping is the task of holding the collective memories and experiences of the community in relationship to God. It is the steady reminder of where we have come from and how we got to where we are. These stories must be regularly recounted in order for traditions and rituals to retain their sacred meaning and for the church to maintain some trajectory of identity and mission. A church without story-keepers is a community without roots. In story-centered renewal, it is imperative that the story the church keeps is not a generic template but rather a particular reflection of its own past and present experiences of being a church.

In 1 Corinthians 9:22, Paul declares that he has "become all things to all people" (NRSV). Many well-meaning Christians have taken Paul's words to be an ideal evangelical strategy. However, Dan McAdams warns that at an individual level, this sort of people-pleasing might actually be dysfunctional: "The protean man or woman is the modern adult who tries to be everything to everybody. Such a person may appear on the surface to be well-rounded and adjusted. . . . But the protean person suffers from a profound inner emptiness. There is no coherence in his or her life. No unifying narrative binds together his or her disparate interests and activities. The self is split, and each part is alienated from the others."[11] It is no less unhealthy for churches, yet many struggling churches seek renewal by trying to offer something for everyone.

This leads to isolated ministries within the church competing with one another for limited resources and a congregation trying to go in multiple directions at once. A bold evangelism approach for Paul has become a bad renewal strategy for a church.

One of the temptations faced by struggling churches attempting to draw in new members is to cast the net as broadly as possible. The goal is to reach anyone and everyone not currently sitting in the sanctuary on a Sunday morning. Oftentimes, this mentality is evident in those insisting upon new programs and events targeting specific demographics present in the macrocommunity but not within the church. The belief is, "If we can prove to [insert specific people group here] that we are their kind of church, then they will come." What often occurs as a result of this mentality and approach to renewal is that in an attempt to be everything to everyone, the church ends up doing none of those things well enough to truly help anyone. Being everything to everyone is not a feasible or functional strategy. No church (no matter how large or wealthy, but especially not a struggling one) has the resources to sustain such a universal ministry. Eventually, the limits of financial and human capital are reached, and choices must be made.

When the "all things to all people" mentality is brought to the search for a new story, the result is much the same. With such an overwhelming variety of stories and such a diverse audience, the church is tempted to tell a story generic enough to appeal to as many potential new members as possible. For instance, "We strive in all we do to love God and neighbor and to serve Jesus Christ." Yes, that story communicates that you are a church, but it does not do anything to differentiate your church from every other church nor does it do anything to focus the mission and ministry of the community. Seth Godin warns against giving in to the broad-net temptation. He writes, "Your tepid, compromised approaches to storytelling—stories that will please everyone, even those who don't want to hear them—are likely to fail."[12] What Godin recommends instead is to be "an extremist in your storytelling."[13] What he means is that the church's story must resonate with particular strongly held beliefs of the congregation and of a particular audience within the macrocommunity. As noted near the end of chapter 1, a congregational story tapping into the church's passion will strike a chord with those who share that passion, whether they count themselves part of the church or not. "Your story doesn't have to be salacious or noisy or over the top. But it must be remarkable."[14] A generic story may not upset or offend anyone, but it is also unlikely to arouse much attention. A particular story, on the other hand, will be more personal to the church and more likely to pique the interest of others. It is a story more likely to resonate. Trying to capture all the stories is the same as having no story, because there is still no single binding narrative—nothing that makes you stand out.

This effort to stand out is the endless quest of branding. For Christian Salmon, story and brand are closely related. He describes a progression in marketing emphases that has shifted from selling a product to selling a brand to, now, selling a story. If we accept the shift described by Diana Butler Bass in which twentieth-century churches adopted a business mentality and began treating religion as their product,[15] then Salmon's progression would indicate the necessity for a twenty-first-century change in the way churches do marketing. Declining membership and giving suggests disinterest in and devaluation of the "product" the church is offering, a problem requiring rebranding through story. Salmon quotes Barbara Stern as saying, "What branding really is, is a story attached to a product. . . . The smart way is to change the value of the product by telling a story about it."[16]

For instance, the United Church of Christ has demonstrated a commitment to the particularity of the story it keeps over the past twenty years while establishing its brand of progressive mainline Christianity. Around the turn of the twenty-first century, understanding the need to distinguish its "product"—its particular expression of Christian faith and practice—from that of other mainline denominations, the United Church of Christ began to tell stories about extravagant welcome that illustrated its theology of grace, a commitment to unity and justice, and a practice of radical hospitality. The kind of stories the UCC told fit the "extreme" label given by Godin. In telling stories about affirming same-sex marriages and ordaining gay clergy, the denomination raised the eyebrows of people both inside and outside church walls. In telling stories about protesting racial injustice, the denomination risked upsetting the overwhelmingly white majority of people in its pews. In telling such extreme stories, the UCC risked and, in the case of more than one congregation, succeeded in alienating a significant number of its current members. Nevertheless, it was and still is committed to telling a clear, particular story of progressive main-line Christian faith in hopes of reaching potential members with whom the story of extravagant welcome and of being a prophetic voice in the nation and world resonates.

The concerted effort made at the denomination's highest level demonstrated the power of a particular story to be both an organizational tool for those considered insiders and an evangelical tool to reach those on the outside. The story of extravagant welcome could serve as both a rallying call and an impetus for outreach. This echoes the previous chapter's discussion of Alcoholics Anonymous, wherein the story of recovery is its greatest unifier, strongest attraction, and most valuable export. As also mentioned in chapter 3, like AA, the United Church of Christ knew it could trust in its polity to balance the extremism of the stories by simultaneously affirming respect for individuality while encouraging communal fidelity.

The UCC recognizes the autonomy of each local congregation within a denominational covenant. What that means in storied terms is that the denomination tells the denomination's story, but it claims neither the authority nor the intention to tell the story of every local UCC church. The polity allows for plurality and diversity. Each local congregation is free to affirm as much or as little of the denominational story as is contextually or relationally appropriate. As a result, the UCC, despite its "extreme" stories, still encompasses a wide-ranging spectrum of political and theological positions among its congregations. The denomination's polity allows that even under the general title of "United Church of Christ," there is room for particularity amid individual churches.

The double-edged sword of such a polity is that no two UCC churches must be the same. At times, it can be challenging and frustrating to reconcile the differences between UCC congregations with contradictory theological and political leanings and who offer dramatically different worship and fellowship experiences. However, story-centeredness offers a way of seeing UCC polity as a blessing rather than a detriment to its transformative mission. Rather than attempting to uniformly dictate a story for any and all churches under the "UCC" banner, the denomination's polity allows each church the freedom for its congregational story to be an organic expression faithful to the particularity of its setting, character, and plot.

Finally, the particularity of extreme stories invites connection at a deeper level than does the safety of generality because it provokes decision. When the United Church of Christ began telling its story of extravagant welcome, many local churches decided the story was too extreme and opted to withdraw from the denomination. Others, while not in full agreement, still affirmed their covenantal commitment. Still others enthusiastically took hold of the story. However particular or extreme the story may be, there must be some element to which a person (or local church) still feels a sense of belonging—that the church's story connects to their lives and that they connect to the community formed by that story. To that end, the way in which the UCC has managed to publicly maintain a particular story and yet functionally be inclusive of many who object to portions of the story is suggestive of how a local congregation might afford to be particular in the story it keeps while being respectful of all its members.

Generic stories are necessary only where there is fear that disagreement will make relationship unsustainable. If approaching story-centered renewal through the AA and UCC dynamics of autonomy and covenant, the church can afford to have a particular, remarkable, extreme story while acknowledging the varying degrees with which that story might resonate with its members, respecting that some may decide they no longer belong and trusting that the relational bond of the community will largely be held together in humility and love.

Questions for Reflection

- Where have you noticed "everything to everyone" tendencies within your church?
- How does your congregation understand its relationship to the larger church? How do members understand their relationship to the body?
- What might be an extreme story particular to your church?

Telling an Authentic (Not Imitative) Story

Storytelling, as Lytle uses the label, is the task of passionately communicating the Story of God and the church's story in such a way as to capture the imaginations and hearts of others and draw them into the drama. The story must be told if new generations are going to seize it for themselves. A church without storytellers lacks the energy necessary for its story to be heard. Storytellers are the "jumanjic" pulsing heartbeat testifying to the life inside. In story-centered renewal, it is crucial that the stories told are authentic reflections of the congregation's own heart and not merely imitative echoes of stories others are telling.

Another consequence of the church's buying into the notion that it must look outside itself for a new story is the impulse to abandon discernment and adopt the first story that promises to attract the most people and money in the short term. Because we are easily distracted, we are prone to latch on to the loudest, shiniest story. (Squirrel!) And because we are competitive, we will want to mimic the story that seems to be working for the growing church down the road. But as Seth Godin warns, "You cannot succeed if you try to tell your competition's story better than they can."[17] The church must find a story that is uniquely its own, which means that not only does the church's story need to be particular, but also it needs to be rooted in who the church genuinely is. That means finding a story that is also authentic.

The true story that only we can tell is the story that distinguishes us from every other person or every other church. Dan McAdams insists of the authentic story that "more than anything else it is what makes you unique."[18] So while the temptation is to imitate successful stories of other churches and adopt them as our own, the more valuable task is to discover the story that is solely ours, because prospective churchgoers are rarely interested in how your church is *like* every other church. Rather, they want to know what makes your church *different*. What is it that is true about you—your identity and your mission—that may not be true about any other church? It is not just another call for particularity but instead a particularity grounded in actuality rather than attractionality—in truth rather than appearances.

In a world of imitation, where the pressure is to become a copy of a copy of a copy and to comply when ordered to pay no attention to the man behind the curtain, people yearn for authenticity. To illustrate this yearning, Annette Simmons tells a short, humorous parable about a parrot's owner making repeated trips to the pet store complaining that the bird will not talk. The store clerk sells him a mirror for the cage, then a bell for the cage. Still no talking. In the end, the disgruntled owner brings the dead bird to the store and reports that before it died, the parrot finally spoke one word: "Food." Simmons connects the short parable to human hunger for authentic stories: "People are starving for meaningful stories, while we are surrounded by impersonal messages dressed in bells and whistles that are story-ish but no more effective than giving a mirror and bell to a starving parrot. People want to feel a human presence in your messages, to taste a trace of humanity that proves there is a 'you' (individually or collectively) as sender."[19] Authenticity moves the church story—even a particular one—from merely story-ish to having the ability to connect on a personal level with others.

Because the church's story is a point of human connection, it is of utmost importance that the story the church tells is true if it is to gain the trust of those who hear it. The generations of those who have grown up in the age of social media and story-centered marketing possess a keen eye and ear for detecting inauthenticity. They are adept at seeing through facades and reading between lines. They sense when the story is more about selling a false image than telling the truth, and no one takes kindly to being lied to. They would rather see dust than polish because at least the dust is honest.[20]

In both chapter 2 and chapter 3, I noted the importance of not omitting darkness or sin from our stories. A church seeking to tell an authentic story tells its whole story—its glories as well as its faults.[21] Stephen Denning uses the sinking of the *Titanic* to illustrate the difference between telling a story that is factually true and telling a story that is authentically true. He suggests that while emphasizing the number of lives saved in the disaster would result in a positive story and one that is still factually true, failing to acknowledge the sadness of the many more lives lost would prevent it from being authentically true.[22] Similarly, many churches (and most individuals) attempt to paint themselves in the most colorful and happiest of lights, pointing out all of their finest moments and grandest achievements. Few, however, include struggles, disappointments, or mistakes in the story they tell of themselves. Authenticity means embracing the good and the bad.

I would add, in light of the *Titanic* example, that authenticity also means not pretending to be something or someone you are not. "Authenticity means owning up to what you are and what you stand for."[23] In terms of authenticity, omission or ambiguity tends to be seen as no less disingenuous than outright lying. Movements like Church Clarity, whose goal is to analyze a church's available literature for a clear understanding of their positions on matters like LGBTQ+ inclusion and women in leadership, have sprouted up out of people's desire for more authentic churches. Those movements won't be going away anytime soon, nor should they.

While there can be short-term benefits to telling an inauthentic story—of selling people on the most perfect version of
yourself—the long-term implications are decidedly negative. Denning anticipates the damage of giving in to the temptation to bend
truth: "Inauthentic storytelling may work in the short term, but it
isn't a sound foundation for any individual, business, or society. If
it is tolerated or even encouraged and taught in schools, whether
by cunning, carelessness, ignorance, indifference, loss of confidence, or an inability to distinguish right from wrong, or by gov-
ernmental fiat, then the society is accordingly impoverished, and
we are all accountable for the loss."[24]

While Denning only intimates at the political ramifications of
inauthentic storytelling, Christian Salmon addresses head-on the
ways in which politicians have learned to use inauthentic stories
rather than truth to win votes. Writing shortly after George W. Bush
was elected to his second presidential term, Salmon's observations
have been further confirmed by subsequent elections. He writes,
"The ability to structure a political vision by telling stories rather
than using rational arguments has become the key to winning and
exercising power in media-dominated societies that are awash
with rumors, fake news, and disinformation."[25] Salmon's words feel
prescient when, in light of the current political and social climate
in America, it seems Denning's fear has been realized: the allure
of power has trumped a commitment to authenticity and truth.
"The successful candidate is the one whose stories connect with
the largest number of voters";[26] and today, candidates seem willing
to tell any story necessary—even intentionally untruthful ones—to
connect. So politicians make empty promises and speak of lofty
visions they have no intention of fulfilling. What makes inauthentic
stories so dangerous is that they cannot and are not meant to lead
to any meaningful action.

Churches *must* rise above such tactics.

Churches, in seeking to connect and attract as many potential
new members as possible, are lured by the same "by any means
necessary" approach to story. But inauthentic storytelling is irre-
sponsible storytelling; and while there may be short-term gains,

the long-term consequence is a breach of trust that may be difficult to repair. The church must resist the temptation to imitate the
tactics of politicians by parroting stories for mass appeal. Instead,
the church must seek to find authentic stories, which will enhance
its credibility. The credibility earned through authenticity is essential if the story is going to impact its receiver.[27] Only authentic stories told by credible tellers can inspire the sort of transformational
action sought by storied Christian communities.

Unlike the inauthentic story, which grows out of the desire
for immediate gains, the authentic story is grounded in actuality with an eye toward lasting impact. For that reason, finding an
authentic story occurs not by imposing a prefabricated story upon
the church but rather by allowing an organic story to emerge from
within. That organic process ensures that the church story will be
grounded in who and what the church currently is rather than a
false sense of who it wants to believe (or wants others to believe)
it is. Moreover, it helps ensure that the story is rooted credibly in
practice. Practice is the best gauge of authenticity. Godin defines
authenticity by declaring, "You are telling the truth when you live
the story you are telling."[28] Story-centered renewal, like marketing, hinges on authenticity because the truth of the story is always
checked by praxis.[29] By finding an authentic story that is close
to its heart, the church increases the likelihood that it will tell a
story it is able to embody in practice.

Questions for Reflection

- What is the danger of telling an inauthentic story?
- What attractive stories are being told by other churches
  in your area?
- What might be an authentic story to your church?

Making a Congruent (Not Manipulative) Story

Story-making is the task of re-creating and reshaping the story through new media and for new audiences. It is story in action. It is the story the church keeps and tells applied to each facet of the church's ministry. A church without story-makers has no way of dreaming up new forms of ministry, nor does it have a standard for determining whether its ministries are faithful to its story. In story-centered renewal, the stories being made must be congruent with one another and with the overarching story of the church; otherwise, the intents and purposes of the ministry will be questioned. The question of a story's congruence is the question of whether the church is demonstrably who its story suggests it is. When the church's story is not congruent with the actual behaviors and beliefs of the church, then it is likely that the story is meant to manipulate the audience for some non–mutually beneficial gain.

Manipulative marketing is a habit the church picked up during the same period when religion was becoming its "product." Denning believes that manipulation of the audience is a major part of the modern business model in which "the customer is treated as a thing to be manipulated to buy the products and services generated by the system."[30] In other words, if you could convince someone they need religion and, more importantly, need to get it at *your* church, then they would show up with their pocketbooks ready. That business model no longer works as reliably as it once did. The customer has more options in the marketplace of goods and services, more readily available information on products and consumer experiences, and more sense than to assume from a guarantee on the box that what's on the inside is worth their money. The tables have turned, and the consumer is now in charge and more attentive than ever to incongruities of story, and "if the story is confusing or contradictory or impossible, the consumer panics and ignores it."[31] Or worse.

One of the intersecting points between Denning's and Salmon's work occurs at the discussion of consumer reactions to the exposure of a story's incongruity. Denning compares the decline in the credibility of the corporate story to the proportionate increase in the power of the consumer story.[32] Salmon addresses that same reversal in writing about "antibrand" movements that have targeted companies like Nike and organizations like the Catholic Church when questions of congruence have been raised.[33] Ordinarily, declining sales or membership numbers would spark the development of a buzzworthy new product or program. But when the loss of customers can be attributed to something hurtful, like unjust labor practices or the systemic cover-up of sexual abuse, it is going to take something more substantial to earn back people's trust. This means that the knee-jerk ploy of changing the color of the carpet, repainting the walls, restaffing, and calling the product "new and improved" will no longer work. Annette Simmons quips, "You can't wallpaper a story of hope, trust, and integrity onto disillusioned, stressed-out, and cynical stories."[34] A congregation that has caused hurt to its community or has suffered trauma itself cannot move forward without repentance and healing. A story of "new and improved" must be congruent with actual congregational change. And the deeper the incongruity, the more difficult that change will be.

Congruence must be a point of concern for the church in finding its story because incongruity will not remain hidden. Also, because incongruity has the potential to undermine the reception of the new story, the first part of any story-finding process must involve some soul-wrenchingly honest self-assessment. In other words, if the church story is to be congruent, it cannot tell only of its future self; it must also tell of its present self. This step is not easy, but it is necessary. According to Simmons, this search for a congruent story and the discovery of hidden incongruity "can test your faith that your organization and your group are basically good people with good intentions who walk their talk."[35] The search for congruence can illuminate the church's shortcomings and hypocrisy in ways that tempt us toward disillusionment. Still, the self-examination must occur because "a story that confuses cannot convince. The congruence of your message demands that all your channels of communication be tuned to the same frequency."[36] In making a resonant church story, there is little room for notes to be sounding off-key.

Denning presents two pairing concepts for understanding where incongruity may occur in organizational life. First, he describes incongruity in terms of the difference between an organization's (or church's) espoused values and its operational values.[37] This is the difference between the ideal values we claim and the actual values influencing our decisions. Incongruity is the disconnect between who we like to *think* we are and who we *really* are. Where the espoused values and operational values of a church do not align, the church's story begins to sound manipulative. For instance, he writes, "In traditional management, the espoused values of collaboration and the operational values at work often exist on opposite sides of a deep gulf."[38] The church may say that every member has equal opportunity to participate in church leadership and ministry, but in practice, the system may quietly exclude newer or younger members in favor of those considered more knowledgeable or more responsible. Or the church may say it believes in the priesthood of all believers but in practice makes clear that there are tasks only the pastor is permitted, or expected, to do.

The other pairing framework Denning uses is that of comparing official stories to covert stories. Like the espoused values, official stories are the publicized accounts of what the organization or church stands for and does. The covert stories, on the other hand, are the ground-level accounts usually shared among members of the community and are often more representative of the operational values. Official stories are broadcast in newsletters and published in meeting minutes; covert stories are told behind closed doors or after meetings in the parking lot. Official/espoused stories are the Pride flag or Black Lives Matter banner displayed outside the church building; covert/operational stories are the bigoted or racist tendencies still harbored in the congregation's hiring practices and mission decisions.

Denning warns, "In an unhealthy organization, dissonance between the covert stories and the official organizational stories will be significant."[39] Where there is incongruity, there is danger. An incongruent story can cause long-lasting damages to the church, so it is imperative that the church be conscious of its incongruities and ensure that its practices are consistent with the new story before the story is told. If the church is to discern its story, it must be on the lookout for incongruities and be willing to work through the dissonance, however trying that might be.[40]

The last question that a discussion of congruence raises is, "Who is in charge of telling the church's story?" This question arises out of the recognition that congruence of message and practice is easier to maintain with fewer stewards of the church story. Salmon supposes that a sort of "storytelling management" could exist, which limits the spread of dissonant covert stories within the organization and prevents nonsanctioned stories from spilling out into the community.[41] However, while that approach may succeed in maintaining a uniform story, it is too susceptible to the abuses of power and the silencing of minority opinions or prophetic voices warned of in chapter 3. Storytelling management can devolve into an institutionally minded entity and totalitarian enterprise that ultimately betrays its own purpose.

Contrary to there being managers of the story, Godin counters by asserting, "Now we know that marketing = storytelling, and everything an organization does supports the story. So everyone is in the marketing department."[42] In other words, there is no clear boundary between who does or does not help make the church's story. Every individual—no matter how young or old, committed or uncommitted—is a part of making it, demonstrating its particularity, living its authenticity, and embodying its congruence. The church story will never belong to a select few. For a congregation to handle any of the story-centered modes Lytle describes, it must wholeheartedly enter into the shared praxis process and be in ongoing conversation and contemplation of the relationship between its story and practices. From discernment to formation to proclamation, from keeping to telling to making, the church story that is particular, authentic, and congruent is never "theirs" but always "ours."

Questions for Reflection

- What, if any, are the lingering negative consumer stories of your church?

- How does your church assess the faithfulness of its ministries and connect them to its overall story?

- Can you name any discrepancies between the church's espoused and operational values or between its official and covert stories?

Integrating Story Centrality

An Individual and Communal Task

So far, I have discussed in previous chapters the existential need for story in the church, the storied nature of Christian faith, the benefit of story-centeredness to the life of a community, and the ways in which story is being employed in other arenas of society. This closing chapter will focus on how a church's story (yours in particular) can be discerned and how storied thinking can be integrated into its congregational life and ministry.[1] But first, it is imperative to acknowledge the personal component of storied faith development so that in our attentiveness to the congregation's overall story, we do not overlook the growth needs of individual members. Implementing story centrality at a congregational level cannot occur at the cost of congregants.

Recall the storytelling triangle (see figure 1.1) and remember the multiple factors at work in the storied life of any particular congregation. External, *setting-related stories* affect the church on a communal and individual plane. Each member brings individual, *character-related stories* into the community. The congregational story itself intersects and participates in the *Story of God*. Because of these multiple story channels, the search for the church story is a "psychosocial activity" wherein the individual and communal are distinct but not separate.[2] There cannot be a communal story that does not take into account the individual experiences of church members, and there cannot be a church story if those individual stories are not also interpreted communally.

Thankfully, whether applied personally or communally, storied development follows a similar trajectory. Figure 5.1 depicts a view of storied development through the shared psychosocial lens of Erik Erikson's study of human development and Dan McAdams's study of the story-making self. In his connection of story-making language to Erikson's categories of psychosocial development, McAdams offers a helpful lens through which to see how the integration of storied faith is also a developmental process. For readers interested in this theoretical fusion, the appendix contains a more thorough articulation of this merger.[3]

Developmental stage	Developmental skill(s)	Story-making skill
Infancy	Trust/hope	Narrative tone
Early childhood	Autonomy/will	Collecting imagery
Late childhood	Initiative/purpose	Narrative themes
Adolescence	Identity/fidelity	Identity
Young adulthood	Relationships/love	Imago
Middle adulthood	Unity/care	Resolution
Late adulthood	Integrity/wisdom	Legacy

FIGURE 5.1. Shared stages of Erikson and McAdams

However, the purpose of this section as a prelude to the rest of this chapter is to stress the developmental character and simultaneous paths (i.e., individual and communal) of storied development. Since story-centered renewal is intended to be participatory and not an imposed system, it will be most effective when as many people as possible are participating in the storied development of the community. Not every individual in the church is at the same place in their faith development or in the development of their personal storied self. Neither will each one be in the same place in their storied faith development. As such, for story-centered thinking to become a holistic approach of the church, it must be applied and practiced in ways that meet each congregant where they are in their personal storied development. Any church leader intent on implementing storied thinking for the sake of congregational renewal must not only be aware of the personal growth taking place but also take into account that not all who gather will grow in the same way or from the same starting point. Therefore, prior to introducing specific ways of implementing storied thinking into the faith and practices of the church, it is essential to present an overview of the various attitudes we may find among our churches and their members when undertaking our search for story. Knowing where we might meet them enables us to make wiser choices in the incorporation of storied thinking and practices.

First, almost every person expresses some innate resistance to change. Churches often express that aversion more strongly. Usually, the anxiety around change is rooted in a fear based on negative prior experiences or uncertainty and mistrust. Some congregations and individuals have had past experiences that make them wary and skeptical of anything new. For these people and their churches, the integration of story-centeredness must begin with efforts to restore trust in the community and the revitalization process. Many of our churches and members will need time to buy into the story-centered approach—to believe the congregational culture can adapt to a new mode of thinking and that the community can become the honest and humble fellowship of faith that story-centeredness requires.

Other churches and individuals may be more open to change but lack the necessary language to envision and articulate the change they would like to see. Biblical literacy often varies significantly across a congregation, and the disparity can impact storied faith development. Story-centeredness will entail increasing biblical literacy in order to establish a shared dialect for communicating identity, theology, and story.

Still others will have begun exploring questions of "What for?" and "To whom?" related to ministry and mission. The prophetic voices within the congregation are likely already stirring. Depending on how long the church has been in the struggle of decline and how passionately those prophets have seen and proclaimed the need for change, some may have grown tired or disillusioned. Story-centeredness offers encouragement by providing a clearer framework for critique and creative solutions.

Some people and churches may be going through periods of acute personal or institutional unrest and transition. On one hand, these liminal spaces are prime opportunities for story-centered introspection and exploration. Nothing demonstrates our need to find a more solid foundation than when the sands we built on are shifting. On the other hand, we cannot ignore the weight people carry in the midst of these unstable times. Change is stressful, so pastoral care is not an optional piece of story-centered renewal. As church leaders, we must be sensitive to the emotional needs of the community lest by appearing unsympathetic we lose its trust.

We must also be aware of the tendency for factions to form as individuals and groups of individuals reach differing conclusions about what the church needs and what revitalization may look like. Outright dismissal or angry outbursts will undermine renewal efforts. Here is where the congregational polity discussed in chapters 3 and 4 is best applied as a guiding principle in that it seeks to hold in balance individual autonomy and corporate unity. If the goal of story-centeredness is the greatest amount of participation, then in situations of division, it means making room for disagreement to be discussed in healthy ways.

Finally, some of our churches and their members are primarily concerned with their institutional future. Certainly, it is the fear of closure that drives many churches' yearning for renewal. As such, the present benefits of story-centered renewal will likely be pushed aside as secondary until people are convinced of its ability to secure a future existence for the church. A story-centered approach affirms the generative heart of the church by redirecting that concern and those energies toward the development of a congregational culture and church story with the potential to transcend the turnover of transient membership and mortality.

Story-centered renewal is simultaneously individual and communal. The congregation, as a whole, and the individual members thereof both exist somewhere along the storied development spectrum. Therefore, finding the church's story involves both train-ing individuals within the church how to think in storied terms and guiding the organization through a discernment of its collective story. Telling the Christian story and the church's story together is an important practice, and while we are born with story-making minds, it is a skill that must be honed and grown as we participate in storying activities that are appropriate to our developmental needs. If we combine what I have described here with the image of Groome's shared praxis cycle, what results is a spiral by which a congregation's exploration and understanding of its communal story become deeper and richer as individuals and the collective group become more versed in storied thinking and the storied faith.

Now that I have stressed the necessity for wise discernment in the implementation of storied church practices, we are now ready to move on to the practices themselves. In the next sections of this chapter, I will focus on four distinct arenas of congregational life and ministry—worship, education, fellowship/organization, and the church building—and the ways in which the church's story can be centered in each arena and thereby contribute to the storied faith development and renewal of the congregation.

Questions for Reflection

- What safeguards are in place for maintaining a balance of both organizational and individual growth?
- How does your church tend to handle change practically and emotionally?
- What obstacles do you foresee preventing maximum participation in story-centered renewal?

The Story of Worship

For most churches, the most opportune time to reach as many members of the congregation as possible is during Sunday wor-ship gatherings. It is typically the time when the greatest number of people are together in one space. Since it is the most regular event and generally evokes the most congregational participation, Jane Rogers Vann argues in her book on worship-centered church renewal, "Worship has become paradigmatic for congregational life in that what is said and done in worship sets the pattern for all other aspects of congregational life."[4] Although I do not disagree with Vann's emphasis on the importance of worship, I would argue that story precedes worship. Story is more crucial because while worship sets the tone for the rest of congregational life, the story around which the church is centered will set the tone for the worship experience. Nonetheless, worship is the most likely setting for storied faith development to occur because of its core place in congregational life and because "[it is] where we hear and learn and internalize the story."[5]

Worship is a time filled with meaning-laden rituals, which means it is a time rooted in story. In their book *Mighty Stories, Dangerous Rituals: Weaving Together the Human and the Divine*, Herbert Anderson and Edward Foley describe the symbiotic relationship between story and ritual in the context of worship: "Storytelling and ritualizing together provide the vehicles for reconnecting God's story with our human stories."[6] Moreover, they argue that as storied creatures, "We are a people who not only narrate meaning-laden stories with our lips but who also perform them with our bodies. Human beings are both storytellers and story ritualizers."[7] Worship is the locus of the ritualized story. Yet much of our Sunday morning worship routine today occurs less out of storied meaning than out of rote subservience to "the way we've always done it."

For a church to centralize its story, it must examine the ways in which the story is ritualized in worship. Examining worship through a story-centric lens requires us to look at the stories conveyed—explicitly and implicitly—by the rituals, as well as looking at the stories left untold.[8] In order for this to happen, however, closer attention must be paid to every facet of the worship experience and its design, and to whether these things are contributors or hindrances to the centering of story.

Examining the storiedness of worship means asking questions of the sanctuary space: "Why display the paraments? Why are there pews and stained glass? Why is there an American flag and a Christian flag flanking the altar?" It means asking questions of the liturgy: "Why make the announcements before the Call to Worship but after the Prelude? What purpose does the Children's Message serve?" It means asking questions of the language: "Why use *sins* in the Lord's Prayer as opposed to *debts* or *trespasses*? What pronouns are used to refer to God?" It means asking questions of decorum: "Who is allowed to receive or serve communion? How are children present and engaged in the sanctuary? Who preaches, and from where?" Furthermore, it means asking questions beyond the worship time itself. The story communicated on Sunday morning begins before the first notes are played or anyone enters the sanctuary. So questions also must be asked regarding parking, accessibility, and signage: "Do people feel welcomed and included in worship?"

Questions like these are essential if worship is to have a more story-centered role in the life of the church because worship offers the most natural context for individual stories, the congregation's story, and God's Story to intersect. It is at that intersection where transformation happens. Anderson and Foley declare, "The future of faith communities depends upon their capacity to foster an environment in which human and divine narratives regularly intersect. More specifically, the future of Christian communities requires that they enable the weaving together of the divine and human in the image of Jesus Christ."[9] The future of our churches depends, in large part, on harnessing the story-centric power of worship to transform the lives of those who gather, the life of the community itself, and the world around it.

One of the increasingly popular ways churches are finding to center story and heighten biblical literacy is by shifting away from a dependence on the Revised Common Lectionary, which has long been a stable foundation for worship planning in many mainline churches, and opting instead for a calendar based on the Narrative Lectionary. As its name suggests, the Narrative Lectionary emphasizes the storiedness and continuity of Scripture over the course of an annual cycle through the Bible. In terms of an overarching structure for worship planning, the Narrative Lectionary is a wonderful story-centric alternative. Nevertheless, there are also practical steps that can be taken to include story within the worship service itself.

Preaching

While the whole of Sunday worship is critical to story-centered renewal, Anderson and Foley argue that the preaching event "is perhaps the most potent vehicle for interweaving the human and the divine."[10] The sermon has long been a main staple of the Protestant worship service. The traditional mode of sermonizing whereby the preacher delivers a carefully crafted spiritual lecture to a quietly listening congregation traces its lineage back to the Enlightenment—with its emphasis on logic and the quest for truth—as well as to the modern elevation of preachers as spiritual experts. Author and pastor Doug Pagitt explores the roots of what he calls the "speaching" model of sermons and concludes that this style of preaching has, not surprisingly, been found to be ineffective and alien in a story-centric world.[11] Rather than fostering storied community traits such as connectivity, vulnerability, humility, and authenticity, this mode of preaching reinforces silence and passivity and isolates community members from one another and from the story itself. This mode of preaching can actually exacerbate the existential despair of people in today's society.[12] Yet congregations have grown so used to the speaching model that they often fail to see the negative impact it has had and continues to have on spiritual formation and church vitality. The church has forgotten that in being the church, it is caught up in a story. Through our fixation on the speaching model, the gospel has too long been communicated as information rather than as a formational storied faith.[13] As such, it is a mode that must be challenged and changed in the worship of a story-centered church.

As an alternative, Pagitt proposes (and I affirm here) what he terms *progressional dialogue*. Progressional dialogue is akin to the serial stories of twelve-step programs except that the theme is usually a particular Scripture passage.[14] The preacher introduces the passage and offers some initial reflections, and then, as in serial stories, community members take turns adding to the collective discussion. By doing away with impassioned monologue, progressional dialogue gives the sermon a conversational, multivocal form that I'd argue is more biblical than the traditional sermon style because it more closely resembles the oral storytelling and midrashic practices of earlier storied faith communities. In fact, progressional dialogue as a preaching model embodies many characteristics of the biblical storied faith described in chapter 2. It roots the sermon event in the covenantal relationship of preacher to congregation and congregants to one another. It interacts with Scripture as a dynamic, rather than fixed, witness to God's word. It localizes the sermon to the specific experiences and needs of the community. And it does all of this while allowing for the tension inherent when dealing in the language of metaphor and in the light of personal differences.

Progressional dialogue is an effort to rehumanize the preaching event of worship by reclaiming the storytelling task of preaching from being an individual act of the preacher to a task of the whole community. It accomplishes this most distinctly by attending to the power dynamics between preacher and congregation and the relationship of each teller and hearer to the story being told.[15] What we discover is that there is a leveling that must occur in the preaching event in order for a church to become a storied community. Progressional dialogue accomplishes this by giving the congregation a voice in every part of the sermon process through an invitation into the many parts of preparation that preachers usually tend to do in solitude.

For instance, every Monday morning, I enjoy sipping a coffee while reading through the next Sunday's Scriptures with a handful of congregants. We discover together in conversation. We pray, reflect, and share insights on the way the texts strike us. Often, participants will come having looked ahead at the texts and done some initial study of their own. As a preacher, it is inspiring to see how the Spirit is speaking to them and through them. Often, they make observations I would not have otherwise considered. This Monday routine helps ensure that the shape and content of the sermon are relevant and resonant to more than just my own life.[16] By including other voices, progressional dialogue functions as a safeguard against the story's being manipulated to fit any one person's agenda. It embodies the belief that the church's story is more full and more faithful when it is told communally.

Moreover, the conversational and inclusive nature of progressional dialogue affords the community a chance to process its story together. Uniformity is not the goal of progressional dialogue any more than it is the goal of the Bible. Rather, the goal is to help "local congregations construct their own stories in order to make sense of the gospel in their particular context."[17] The sermon becomes a conversation among friends. It is simultaneously "a way for [someone] to continue processing what's happened in her life within the context of a community she loves and trusts,"[18] in conversation with God's story, and a way to process what the Scriptures mean for the church's story and ministry.

For instance, in an effort to help PUCC think about its own metaphors and story, I designed a progressional dialogue summer worship series looking at the biblical metaphors for the church shown in figure 5.2.

As mentioned in chapter 2, the Bible is rich with metaphors that the people of God have found helpful over time for articulating their identity and purpose. Each metaphor captures different aspects of who the people are and what they do, and each metaphor carries with it its own positive and negative connotations. And while the Church universal is broad and diverse enough to embody all of those metaphors, local churches tend to resonate with one or two more deeply than the rest.

Throughout the summer series, each Sunday centered on a single metaphor. I would begin the progressional dialogue sermon by introducing that Sunday's metaphor in the context of its Scripture passage, offer a few reflections, and then invite the congregation into a discussion of the metaphor's meaning, strengths, and

Metaphor	In Bible	Characteristics	Strengths	Challenges
Fortress	Ps 18	Strong, sturdy, protection from enemies	Trustworthy, secure, confident	Insular, defensive, building-centric
City on a hill	Matt 5:14–16	Model of goodness, beacon to others	Community-minded, praxis emphasis	Self-righteousness, hypocrisy
Mother/ midwife	Rom 8:18–25	Patient, expectant, groaning for new	Life-giving, brave, steadfast, creative, nurturing	Requires self-sacrifice and risk taking
Refuge	Ps 31:1–5	Safety from storms of life	Hospitality, justice, compassion	Building-centric, situational
Table	Luke 22:14–30	Providing for the hungry, intimate	Hospitality, sharing, service-minded	Limited space/ resources, gluttony, pride
Salt of earth	Matt 5:13	Preserves, noticeable influence on world	Community-minded, praxis emphasis	Burnout, pride, hypocrisy
Mustard seed/yeast	Matt 13:31–33	Small but full of transformative potential	Empowering, hospitality, emphasis on everyday acts	Small scale, slow results, hard to undo missteps
Bride	Rev 19:6–9	Covenantal, joyful, partners with God	Person-centric, loving, sharing	Unfaithfulness, broken promises
Tabernacle	Heb 8:1–7	Sacred place of worship, encounter God	Holiness, worship-minded	Exclusive, rigid formality, building-centric
Family	Mark 3:31–35	Relational, loving, loyal	Person-centric, close-knit, caring	Insular, mistrust, dysfunction
Body	1 Cor 12:12–27	Diversity in mutuality	Person-centric, unity, respect	Illness, disease, brokenness

FIGURE 5.2. Biblical metaphors for church

challenges, as well as its relevance to the church's understanding of its own identity and mission. The series engaged the whole community in arriving at a family-table focus.[19] Based on its village church legacy, the church has seen and still does see itself as a family-oriented congregation. Additionally, based on the free community meal the church hosts each month and its enthusiastic support of the local food pantry, the metaphor of the table is also prominent in its self-understanding. Having discerned in such a communal way those two central biblical metaphors, story-centered renewal suggests seizing upon them and organizing the congregation's language, life, and ministry around being a family-table church.

Progressional dialogue allows the preaching event to be a place of communal storytelling, but it is not the only avenue for incorporating other voices and other stories in worship.

Testimony

Another approach to decentralizing the professionalized sermon and inviting the perspectives and voices of others is the practice of sharing testimonies. Some readers may balk at just the mention of the word, so it is important at the outset to clarify what is meant by *testimony*. As a result of their usage within the more Evangelical traditions of American Christianity, testimonies are popularly understood as a recounting of an individual's past life of sin, moment of salvation, and new life in Jesus Christ. They share many similarities with the function and structure of the drunk-a-log in Alcoholics Anonymous. Storytellers will tell of past misdeeds, leading to a rock-bottom moment, followed by a born-again commitment to change, and a description of the transformed life they presently live. However, many mainline Protestant churches are uncomfortable with this sort of "testimony" because of the way that it seems to necessitate the experience of hitting rock bottom and being born again in one's faith journey. The "lost and found" structure is not always relevant to the journey of mainline congregants, many of whom have spent their whole lives in the church and therefore who may recall neither a time they have felt lost nor a moment they have suddenly felt found. Rebecca Anderson, pastor at Gilead Church in Chicago, which includes storytelling moments in its worship service, is careful to distinguish her church's practice from this concept of testimony: "The classic shape of religious testimony . . . is 'I once was lost and now I am found,' but there are lots of stories that are 'I once was lost and I'm still kind of a mess.'"[20] The storytelling that Gilead practices, and that I am suggesting be a part of story-centered renewal, is one that allows for the mess.

Testimony, the way it is being used henceforth, refers less specifically to the story of one's salvation—although that story is a part of this definition—but more broadly to stories of God's activity in one's life or, as Lillian Daniel defines it, "your spoken story about how you had experienced God, offered in the context of our community worship."[21] There are several ways in which testimony, by that broader definition, may be a healthy alternative to progressional dialogue for congregations not yet past the infancy stage as well as for congregations like PUCC who have a cultural preclusion or learned discomfort toward speaking out during worship. Unlike the spontaneity of progressional dialogue, the space testimony affords for selectivity and preparation of the story may make it a more accessible story-centered practice for mainline congregations.

In her book, Daniel describes the methodical incorporation of testimony into the worship and ministry life of a Congregational church in New England that helped transform the community from one of quiet reverence to enlivened proclamation. She recalls that the practice began during a stewardship campaign as a way of breaking down the defensiveness often associated with church finances, and the testimonies were called "giving moments" and were stories about something God had done in the lives of the tellers through the church's ministry. In my own ministry settings, I have incorporated testimony during stewardship campaigns and also during other seasonal occasions in worship life like youth-led services or the lighting of the Advent wreath candles, where each week I asked volunteers to not only do a short reading but also share a brief story about what that week's theme—Hope, Peace, Joy, Love—means to them personally.

The practice of testimony contributes to both personal and communal storied development. It can be empowering for those who share. Daniel muses, "You cannot invite people to tell their faith stories to one another and then be surprised when they become spiritual leaders of the church, and then, spiritual leaders to one another."[22] By welcoming their voices and resisting the urge to pre-view, revise, or otherwise control the content of the testimonies, worship leaders communicate trust and confidence in the laypeople. As in progressional dialogue, the inclusion of others' voices fosters an atmosphere of honesty and hospitality.

Moreover, just as drunk-a-log stories in AA are not merely to benefit the teller but also to help draw new members into the narrative of recovery, testimonies are about both the telling and the hearing: "Listening to testimony helps us to find our thread in God's fabric, and to know that we are never alone in our journeys."[23] In that regard, testimonies are an opportunity for cross-generational conversation, in which newcomers to faith and new members to the congregation can hear how God has been moving while older or longtime members can hear how God continues to move in new ways. For the congregation practicing testimony, there is a built-in corrective whereby the church story is constantly being retold in past, present, and future terms. The "Why?" is continually being reiterated for new ears and new days.

Even if the congregation decides it is not ready for progressional dialogue or testimony and is not ready to depart from the pattern of the pastor as the primary storyteller during worship, there are other ways to enhance worship's story-centeredness.

Liturgy

Despite literally meaning "the work of the people," worship liturgy has seldom been that. Rarely has liturgy been any more participatory or connected to congregants' lives than the sermon.

"Rituals can often become 'disconnected' from our lives, some-times because the primary focus is simply to repeat them as 'the tradition.' Stories of contemporary lives and brokenness often do not appear in the liturgy."[24] Like the critique of classic testimony or children's literature, liturgy seldom seems to leave room for the darkness or messiness of life. Not only does this risk rendering the liturgy irrelevant, but it also makes it dishonest. Anderson and Foley caution, "A ritual is dishonest when its statements do not match the real-life experience of the participants," and "rituals that do not acknowledge the painful or parabolic cannot sustain an honest narrative."[25] Therefore, even if the congregation is not ready to hear the voices of others in the context of worship, it must at least attempt to echo their experiences in the story worship tells through its liturgy.

The difficulty is that the worship services of most churches are designed to focus on generalities so that they might be applicable to as many of the gathered people as possible rather than acknowl-edging the particularities each one brings. In worship, more often than not, the communal story takes precedence over the individual stories. Story-centered liturgy, to the contrary, is more inclusive of congregants' stories. Story-centered liturgy is grounded in the belief that "all human stories are potential windows to the story of God" and, as such, should be doors through which an individual can enter into the story being told in worship.[26] Therefore, it seeks to provide "a place for each human tale and ritual resonance in the ordinary rhythm of Sunday worship with the lives of all wor-shipers," even if that tale involves hurt.[27] To name the broken and hurting places is to invite worshippers into the good news story of redemption, healing, and transformation. The instinct as wor-ship planners is often to control the tone of the worship service by sticking to generalities and avoiding subject matter or buzzwords likely to evoke an emotional reaction. However, while doing so may maintain the lukewarm temperature of the sanctuary, it fails to engage the stories people have brought with them into the worship space. To refuse to name the fear or hurt or concern is to suggest by omission that it is outside the reach of God's grace.

The integration of worshippers' stories can occur through the use of inclusive language, acknowledgment of current events in the community and in the world, and opportunities for reflection and intercessory prayer. One of the more powerful ways to bring the stories of the people into the context of worship's story is by allowing space for extemporaneous prayers to be offered either by inviting requests to be made or by providing time for silence. Vann writes, "If reflection on experience is a way of telling our own stories back to ourselves, then prayer is in part telling our stories to ourselves and to God."[28] Prayer is an underutilized avenue into story-centered worship.

Additionally, recall that Lillian Daniel began using testimony in her congregation during stewardship because they discovered that the call to give took on a different tone when it was story-centered. When each part of the liturgy feels connected to the overall story of worship—when each worship service feels connected to the overall story of the church—people are less likely to disengage. Points in the liturgy such as offering and announcements feel less like tangential excursions into the business side of church life when they are incorporated into the story of worship and the stories of the people. For example, build the reminder about the upcoming food drive into the sermon. Include the call to outreach in a prayer of confession. Or make the capital campaign for parking lot repair a story of hospitality. Take advantage of opportunities, whenever they present themselves, to make every piece a part of the whole story.

Finally, the sacraments the church celebrates, while special to every church, bear even more meaning to the story-centered church. "Christians are a story-formed people, formed after the likeness of Jesus Christ through the continual remembrance of his life, death, and resurrection," and our sacraments are a key part of the church's common memory because they are a means of establishing that Christian community and identity.[29] Inasmuch as sacraments recall the memory of who and *whose* we are, they are essential to story-centered worship. Both of those sacraments recognized by most mainline Protestant churches—baptism and communion—are brimming with story and imagery that have profound resonance in a story-centered community. Yet because of the rigidity and formality often associated with them, the celebration of the sacraments too often becomes a case of ritual detached from story and reality. For instance, Mary McClintock Fulkerson and Marcia W. Mount Shoop, in their book A *Body Broken, a Body Betrayed*, laud the vision-shaping potential of eucharistic practices but lament the dissonance between a church's practices of communion and the church's story, arguing that sanitized rituals miss out on the subversive potential of the sacrament. Instead, they put forth a story-centric vision of eucharistic practice that "invites its practitioners to connect to Jesus' words and stories in ways that change who we are and how we live in the world today."[30] The tone of communion should be different on any other Sunday in Advent than it is on Christmas. The joy of an Easter communion meal doesn't belong at Table on Maundy Thursday. The global unity of the Church proclaimed on Worldwide Communion Sunday—the first Sunday of October in many mainline churches—seems less significant if we haven't taken time to address the real division and disunity that exists in our world. Lifting up the broken body of Christ can be an opportunity to lift up the names of contemporary victims of state-sponsored violence, religious extremism, and political expedience.

The practices of baptism and communion always tell a story, but frequently those stories have nothing to do with the overall story of worship, the story of the church, or the stories of the people gathered in worship. The connection that the sacraments have to the story of worship and to the church's story provides opportunities to engage participants in the story in tangible ways. For example, I have begun inviting the children of whatever congregation I am serving to help bless the baptismal waters during the sacrament of baptism in order to involve them in the story and remind them of their place in the storied community. Also, as mentioned earlier, PUCC had voted to open the communion table to all who gather in worship regardless of membership or age so that anyone in the family might partake. While leadership took time to wrestle responsibly with the theological arguments on either side of the decision, they ultimately chose to emphasize hospitality and inclusion as foremost to the story being told by the church in worship and in general. The open table of communion was an early manifestation of the church's family-table story in worship. However, regardless of the central metaphors of the church, its sacraments can be signposts pointing to both Christ and the guiding story by which the church understands itself as embodying Christ's mission.

Worship has such a primary place in story-centered renewal because it is "a shared communal practice that enables the community to tell its own story again and again" and "serves as an 'undercurrent' that provides energy and direction for congregational life."[31] A story-centered church must consider the elements of its worship and how they help or hinder the telling of its story.

Questions for Reflection

- How important is worship in the overall life of your church?

- What kind of preaching style is used in your context? How engaged are congregants in the sermon?

- How relevant are the liturgy and sacraments to the life of the church and the daily lives of its people?

The Story of Education

A second major area of congregational life that impacts its story-centeredness is the area of teaching or Christian education. A significant number of the forerunners in storied church thinking have come out of backgrounds in Christian education. That is not coincidental. As demonstrated earlier in the chapter, there is a significant degree of overlap between spiritual growth and story.

Sunday School

For many mainline churches, the traditional means for accomplishing Christian education is through a Sunday school model, whereby students are arranged according to age and taught in classrooms using a carefully designed curriculum. The timing of Sunday school varies from church to church. Some opt to have Christian education take place before, after, or between Sunday morning worship services, some during. For many churches, Sunday school has been an unquestioned essential of congregational life since churches began to function as learning centers charged with the task of equipping members with proper doctrine and lifestyle.[32] However, the decline in church attendance and membership has meant a decline in Sunday school numbers as well. As such, the efficacy of the traditional Sunday school model is dwindling to the point that many churches have begun looking at the traditional model and asking what could be done better or whether there is any use in continuing to use the Sunday school model at all.

In many cases, Sunday school classes are divided by age and isolated from one another, and the question has been asked, "Why, if families spend so much time apart from one another during the week, would they want to come to church and be separated again?" In response to that question, some churches have begun utilizing curricula created for intergenerational groups. However, these intergenerational curricula can sometimes suffer from the same pitfalls as our attempts at the generalized application of worship; that is, in trying to fit everyone, they engage no one.

Another critique of the traditional model has been the fluidity of curricula. Christian publishing companies are constantly generating new curricula in an attempt to keep up with ebbing and flowing cultural and learning trends. As a result, there tends to be very little consistency from year to year or class to class throughout a church's Sunday school ministry. Age-defined classes each have their own curriculum, and what a student learns one year rarely has much carryover to the following year.

In looking at the Sunday school dilemma through story-centric eyes, the questions become, "How might the traditional Sunday school model be transformed into a vehicle not just for knowledge but also for transmitting the storied faith of the storied community?" Story-centered Christian education begins with the assertion that just as preaching needs to cease being "speaching" and become more multivocal, the educational process must become less lecturing and more dialogical in form. Professor Anne E. Streaty Wimberly presents the term *story-linking* to talk about the educational process of intentionally connecting the life stories of participants to the storied Christian faith of both Scripture and tradition. "The purpose of this linkage," she writes, "is to help persons be aware of the liberating activity of God and God's call to vocation—living in the image of Jesus Christ—in both biblical and present times."[33] She describes four phases of the story-linking process:

1. Engaging the everyday story by considering the experiences and agenda a person brings to the storied faith and how those stories are impacted by identity, social setting, relationships, and so on.[34]

2. Engaging the Christian faith story in the Bible "through contextual lenses."[35]

3. Engaging Christian faith stories from our heritage and tradition.

4. Engaging in Christian ethical decision-making.

I agree with Wimberly that these four phases of story-linking are critical to faith development and therefore must become foundational aspects of Christian education in the story-centered church.

By incorporating those four phases and drawing from Fowler's stages of faith development and the age-appropriate expectations, I developed a story-centered Sunday school structure in which classes were divided into five age groups with progressive faith development and story development goals (see figure 5.3). The Seeds of Growth curriculum follows a three-year cycle through the Bible so that as students move from one class to the next, the subject matter is repeated, only with different developmental goals.

Class	Age range	Faith development	Story development
Pods	6–8	Learning environment, Bible stories/ characters	Narrative tone, imagery
Sprouts	9–11	Elements of worship, basic Christian concepts	Narrative themes
Buds	12–14	Navigating the Bible and how to study it	Attention to context and exploration
Blooms	15–17	Application of biblical principles to life	Identity, imago
Oaks	18–99+	Biblical criticism, engaging complex topics, respecting diversity	Identity, imago, resolution

FIGURE 5.3. Seeds of Growth

Admittedly, the Seeds of Growth structure resembles the basic structure of the educational curricula designed to accompany the use of the Narrative Lectionary. Certainly, if a congregation has determined it appropriate to their storied development to utilize the Narrative Lectionary in its worship planning, then using the coinciding curriculum makes perfect sense. However, Seeds of Growth originated independently of the Narrative Lectionary and therefore offers enough of a variation to be a learning tool for congregations whose worship planning remains independent of its educational curricula.

Here is a brief example of the Seeds of Growth structure: In week one of year one, every class does a lesson on Genesis 1 and 2. The Pods class learns about God, Adam and Eve, and the order of creation. The Sprouts class learns about God as "Creator" and Sunday as a "day of rest." The Buds class compares the two creation accounts and talks about genre. The Blooms class discusses what it means to be created "in the image of God" and entrusted with the care of creation. Finally, the Oaks class considers the story in terms of historicity and etiology and wrestles with how it continues to influence debates about creation care and the institution of marriage.

The story-linking intent of each lesson is twofold. First, there is the trust that because each lesson is developmentally appropriate, the student will be able to connect the biblical story to their life experience in some way. Second, there is the hope that because each class is looking at the same biblical story, there will be an intergenerational dialogue between family members or church members who attend different classes. The implementation of story-centered Sunday school curriculum and the achievement of those two intentions will lead to the greater development of storied faith and storied community.

Small Groups

Outside of Sunday school, small group studies like Bible studies or book studies are a second popular mode of Christian education and typically occur on days and times other than Sunday mornings. Small group studies are often designed with a particular audience and learning goal in mind. Historically, small group studies in mainline churches have tended to be intensely exegetical Bible studies led by the pastor. These advanced classes were a consequence of the same emphasis on knowledge that produced the traditional model of Sunday school, and often, despite contributing to biblical literacy, they did little to tether the Bible to attendees' hearts or lives to the storied faith, nor did they do much to connect the Scriptures to the church's overall identity and mission. Story-centered small group studies take a different path.

If approached with an eye toward storied faith development, small group studies can be prime opportunities for growth because of the greater level of depth and intimacy that can be achieved. In story-centered renewal, small group studies become less about attaining extra information and knowledge and instead become more about developing eyes to see the stories around us and in our own lives as they intersect with God's Story. And these small groups invite voices to share those stories with one another. At PUCC, we looked at a book that helped the group consider the Bible through the lens of storied faith.[36] We looked at a book that helped the group see biblical values and Christian theology expressed through literary fiction.[37]

Some of the most profound breakthroughs of storied development have occurred in the context of film study groups. Watching movies during a monthly film study group has helped members of the group appreciate film as a medium for storytelling and communication, and also helped them practice story-linking by noting connections between the films, their faith, and their everyday experiences. Movies, because they communicate through story rather than prose, can function as more comfortable entry points into otherwise controversial or complex subject matter than confronting it directly. For instance, a discussion on the topic of religious pluralism and the truth of the Bible benefits from a prelude as beautiful and poetic as *Life of Pi*. Or I have used both *The Truman Show* and *Stranger Than Fiction* as invitations into deep theological reflections on the tension of God's sovereignty and human free will. Film and television are such a regular presence in peoples' lives that it behooves us as churches to harness their power not just as referential signals of cultural relevance but as tools for storied development.

Youth Ministry

Another focal point of many congregations in search of revitalization is the church's youth and children's ministries. Churches pour valuable time and resources into toys, snacks, stunts, and recreational outings in hopes of attaining the interest of kids and teens and thus retaining them and their families in the church. Sadly, these ministries frequently fall into an attractional mindset that values novelty and entertainment over substance. But fun does not have the enduring magnetism that a compelling story does. Once youth outgrow the appeal of lock-ins, kickball, and Chubby Bunny, it is a sense of belonging in the communal identity and mission that will keep them coming back.

Through the storied church lens, youth and children's ministries signify a congregation's investment in the future of its story. The church must ask what story it is communicating. Is it passing along a consumerist, individualistic version of the faith? Or is it telling about a unique community that shares a common story and purpose in God? Story-centered youth and children's ministries seek to escape the attractional trap and attend to the way in which children and teens are grown and guided into the storied Christian faith and the storied church community. Part of this growth and guidance depends on the engagement and vision of adult leaders for the purpose of the youth ministry. For adult leaders, minister-ing with the youth ought to be part of their late adulthood quest for generativity—an opportunity to relay the church's legacy to the next generation of church members not in a patronizing way but in a way that effectively reaches out with a hand of inclusion.

Therefore, while youth-specific meetings, retreats, and activ-ities are important for the spiritual growth needs of youth, it is equally if not more important that the church find ways to include its youth in the overall ministry life of the church. Give them regu-lar opportunities to lead and create worship—more than the annual Youth Sunday or Christmas pageant. Allow them to contribute their voices and ideas to leadership boards and committees. Don't just teach them the church's story for some future telling but invite them and trust them to help shape and tell it in the present.

Confirmation

Along those same lines, it is worth addressing another practice of most mainline churches—Confirmation. It is customary in many mainline churches for youth between middle school and high school age to undergo a catechism process at the end of which they confirm for themselves the promises made at their baptism. The Confirma-tion process and curricula tend to be rigorously academic, an unfor-tunate side effect of which is that the actual Confirmation feels more like a graduation from church than a deepening relationship with it. Across mainline denominations, there is a disturbing trend of youth being confirmed and then disappearing from church life. I believe it is because in all the theology and creeds they learned throughout the catechism process, we fail to connect them to the story.

If baptism marks the initiation into the storied faith and into the storied community, then Confirmation ought to be an affirmation of the individual's intent to continue participating in that story. Like sermons and like Christian education, Confirmation should be less about conveying information and more about catching others up in God's Story. It should prepare confirmands not to graduate from church but to become passionate, contributing members to the story the church is telling.

At PUCC, we revamped the Confirmation process to reflect this greater emphasis on story and discipleship. We condensed the timeline from two years to one year. We utilized as "requirements" as many regular parts of church life as we could as opposed to additional classes in which participation would end as soon as they are confirmed. By encouraging regular attendance at Sunday school and worship, we were hoping to instill lasting habits of faith development. Last, we broadened the target audience and scope of the class to include not only middle school and high school youth seeking Confirmation but also adults seeking to become a new member of the church and current members wishing to reaffirm their commitment to the church. The yearlong process culminated during Holy Week when participants symbolized their commitment to discipleship and service by leading a Maundy Thursday foot washing during worship. Then on Easter Sunday, the congregation celebrated the journey these individuals had undertaken and their respective promises to join their lives to God's Story and the church's story.

Questions for Reflection

- What are your church's current Sunday school and Confirmation structures? How do they foster storied faith and storied community development?

- What small group subjects would your church find most interesting right now?

- If your church has a youth ministry, is it more attractional or discipleship minded?

The Story of Fellowship and Organization

In the village church model, being a locale for fellowship was one of the church's chief purposes. The church was the central hub for families to gather and socialize. Yet, as noted earlier, the frequency and scope of fellowship in village churches have waned as isolationism has increased. That loss of fellowship has no doubt helped accelerate the loss of story. Not only do churches spend too little time together as a church community, but even when we are making time for fellowship, the time spent is seldom story-centered.

Recovering the story and renewing the church require us to restore the practice and focus of fellowship. Congregational renewal will require not just increased fellowship time but also the qualitatively better substance of that fellowship time. Many mainline churches, especially those like PUCC who trace their roots back to German ancestry, are known for their potluck smorgasbords. However, the fellowship of story-centered renewal not only involves food but also calls for the center of that fellowship to be the telling and sharing of stories.

That fellowship may take the form of regular postworship fellowship time with snacks, but it might also mean being intentional about introducing conversation prompts to foster story sharing. Especially in a congregation that may not yet be ready or comfortable with progressional dialogue or testimony, which fosters story-linking during worship, inviting opportunities for personal reflection on worship in a more casual context is imperative. Postworship fellowship affords such a forum.

Story-centered fellowship may also take the form of a periodic event modeled after The Moth story-slam competitions, in which individuals are invited to tell short, original stories based on a common theme in front of an audience. Similar to serial stories in AA communities, such an event would feature diverse reflections on a single topic, invite creativity on the part of tellers, and highlight the unique perspective that each one's lived experience brings to their story.

Regardless of its form, in a story-centered church, fellowship occurs with story at its core. Story gives shape to any instance of a congregation's time together, even time that is dedicated to the more mundane organizational concerns and decisions. Leonard Sweet expounds on the sacredness of the church table when he writes, "The communion table in the sanctuary, and the table of communion in the fellowship hall—both are Lord's Tables."[38] I would add that the board-meeting table is the Lord's table too. A tendency of churches that have lost the storiedness of their faith and community is the detachment of the church's "business" from its spirituality. Particularly when institutional concerns of membership and finances are at the forefront of the minds of leaders, the temptation is to make those concerns the focal point of meetings rather than to center meetings around the telling of the church's story. To counter that temptation, a church might consider conducting its annual congregational meeting in the fellowship hall over lunch with members seated at tables and able to see one another (a setup communicating equality and conversation) instead of holding it in the sanctuary with members all seated facing forward (a posture that reinforces power hierarchies and distance between leadership and laity).

Furthermore, the organizational language of businesses and the institutional church can be translated into the dialect of story. Annette Simmons discusses six types of story a person can tell, each of which has a clear parallel to the organizational life of a church.[39] The first two types she lists are "Who I am" and "Why I am here" stories, which parallel identity and purpose. These types of story are the most fundamental to story-centered renewal and so have already received due attention. The third type of story is teaching stories, which are testimonies supporting the identity and purpose. In the context of a church meeting, teaching stories can be offered as valuable reminders of the blessings that have occurred in members' lives and in the community when the church has been who God called it to be. Vision stories, the fourth type, are the stories looking to what the church is becoming—"a future story that pulls us in."[40] This is the story that should begin each organizational meeting to frame the decision-making and guide the conversation. The fifth type of story is the "value-in-action" story, which parallels mission. These are examples of what the church is doing right now to fulfill its identity and purpose and move toward its vision. In meetings, these stories emerge when the people gathered are given opportunities to share where, in the life of the church, they have recently seen God present or God's work being done. However, "value-in-action" stories can also serve a corrective function if recent stories are hard to come by or if the values being enacted are contradictory to one another or to the church's overarching story—for instance, if the church board has begun the meeting with an affirmation of its vision story to be a church that provides for the needs of its wider community but then does not have any value-in-action stories to tell of current community-support ministries the church is doing. Finally, Simmons lists "I know what you're thinking" stories, which should accompany any new idea or potentially controversial decision because these stories are essentially evangelistic. They reach across to would-be opposition in an attempt to name their possible objection and honor their opinion. Because organizational meetings tend to carry the most weight and tension of decision-making, they also tend to be an arena for conflict in the midst of congregational change. In the midst of conflict or controversy, these "I know what you're thinking" stories become critical for maintaining the health of the community while also not neglecting to make important decisions.

The Story of the Building

Though much of story-centered renewal emphasizes the human qualities of the church, an overview would not be complete without attending to a beloved inanimate aspect of most mainline Protestant churches: the building, which, as much as anything spoken or printed, also tells a story about the congregation that gathers there. Peter Block writes, "Every room we occupy serves as a metaphor for the larger community that we want to create."[41] In other words, the church building and every room in it—from the sanctuary to the signage and the fellowship hall to the restrooms—are part of the story the church tells.

One of the first things I did shortly after beginning my pastorate at PUCC—while I still had an outsider's view—was to walk through the church building and take notes on what story it told me. I then conducted a subsequent tour with the members of its property committee, and while we walked, I asked them questions about decor, accessibility, and overall design.

Leonard Sweet mentions that every piece of furniture and artwork in his home has a story to it and that if at any point no one can remember what the story is, the item is replaced.[42] In surveying the artwork and artifacts adorning hallways, walls, and windowsills of our churches, I would suggest Sweet's housecleaning metric be applied: "Do we still know the story behind it?" Or, better yet, "Does it contribute to the story we are telling?" On my tour with PUCC's property committee, I asked to hear the origin story and significance behind the matchstick replica of the church whose encasement takes up a five-by-five-foot corner of the fellowship hall. My favorite decor discovery, however, was not a revelation that came courtesy of the committee. Rather, there was a crocheted rendition of da Vinci's *The Last Supper* hanging just inside the narthex doorway whose origin none of them could explain. Instead, the answer walked through that narthex door the following day when the last living son of the woman who had made it stopped by the church while in town on business to see what had become of his mother's art. His account of her passion for the craft, her connection to the church, and her insistence that the piece be gifted to the church decades before gave the crochet a storied significance it did not possess two days prior.

I asked them questions about accessibility. Like many churches built in its era, the sanctuary is on the second floor. While the church has installed a chair lift to provide assistance in that regard, neither the men's nor the women's bathrooms are wheelchair accessible. I pushed them to think about what message that sends and what alterations or provisions could be made to counteract accusations of ableism. We proclaim with our lips and literature that "all are welcome here," but does the inaccessibility of the building tell a different story?

Without inundating them with technical jargon, I asked them questions to get at the issue of design. I asked about the layout and the usage of space, like why the junior high Sunday school class gets interrupted every week when people arriving for worship must walk through their classroom in order to reach the sanctuary. I suggested that perhaps either the sanctuary space currently reserved for a glass case of assorted memorabilia or the empty choir loft would be better utilized as a "prayground" area in which younger members of the community could quietly play or color during worship rather than being relegated to the first-floor nursery. Or, since the church has seized upon the family-table metaphors, perhaps the communion table should take on a more prominent place not only in worship but also in the physical design of the sanctuary. I challenged them to think about congruence in building design and decisions: Would the inclusion of technological assets like projection screens contribute to the story or distract from it?

The building may not have an audible voice, but it speaks volumes about the church's story. For a church to fully center its story, it will have to subject its building design to the story rubric: do our church buildings help or hinder the telling of the church's story?

Questions for Reflection

- What opportunities for story-sharing are there in your church's fellowship or meeting times?

- What story does your church building tell? Is it congruent with your church's story?

- What physical changes might faithfulness to the story require?

Conclusion

The path to revitalization for any church is by no means simple, quick, or easy. Congregational change is as complex as the combination of factors that contribute to its decline. But through story-centered renewal, our mainline congregations can overcome the institutional and spiritual despair plaguing them. Each of our churches can reconnect with the storied nature of the Christian faith, reflect more deeply on its place as a community within a larger community, and rediscover its unique role in the Story of God's redemptive work. Moreover, with story-centered thinking, we will have the tools we need to continue revising and recasting its story with each new experience and change that comes around the corner.

Appendix

Stages of Storied Development

Placing the search for story in the category of psychosocial activity implies not only that there are both individual and communal aspects at work but also that the integration of story-centeredness in the church is a developmental process akin to Erikson's theory of human development, McAdams's development of the storied self, and James W. Fowler's theory of faith development.[1] The framework for understanding storied development (see figure 5.1) is a fusion of both individual and communal processes. In this appendix, I offer a more thorough definition of the various stages and, more importantly, their role in storied church revitalization.

Infancy and Narrative Tone

Narrative tone refers to the underlying optimism or pessimism of a story. With regard to congregational culture, it asks, "What is the general 'feel' of things? Is there a sense of excitement and joy in the community, or is it more an atmosphere of guardedness and sadness? What may be causing things to feel that way?" Narrative tone is linked to the infancy stage of human development because of the role that trust has in fostering that general feel of hopefulness. If we cannot trust the church or one another in community, the humility and honesty required of story-centered ministry will not be attainable.

For a congregation in the infancy stage, it will be important to uncover and deal with any past trauma that inhibits it from being a hopeful or trustworthy community. Have there been failed efforts at revitalization before? Have there been staff scandals or massive membership exodus? If so, how has the congregation dealt with the pain? Has the grief been named? Have the sources of conflict been identified and corrected so that healing can occur? The infancy stage emphasis on trust will also require the church to consider to what lengths it goes to ensure that it is a safe environment for all who enter into it. The integration of story-centeredness will go no further than the trust and hope the congregation has in itself and the process.

However, narrative tone is as much about what influence the past exerts on present attitudes as it is also about the assumed trajectory of the story the church understands itself as having. James Hopewell describes four basic trajectories of congregational story—comic, romantic, tragic, and ironic—each of which lends itself to a different tone.[2] Comic stories have a clear, ordered path toward harmony and are by far the most optimistic. A church with a comic tone understands itself as organizationally oriented to God's redemptive Story and destined to thrive. Romantic stories move toward harmony but along a less predictable path. A church with a romantic tone is optimistic but understands itself as relatively disorganized and unfocused. Tragic stories have a clear, ordered path, but that path leads to decay rather than fruitfulness. A church with a tragic tone understands itself as having a purpose, but that purpose is to fight a losing battle in a rebellious world. Ironic stories are devoid of either order or meaningful resolution. A church with an ironic tone laments with Qoheleth, "Meaninglessness, meaninglessness, everything is meaningless!" This is the resignation heard in the complaint, "It doesn't matter what we do; none of it will ever work."

It is possible for churches to shift from one tonal story to another. For instance, while the lack of past trauma allows for trust and hope and a sense of order, the longer a church like PUCC goes without seeing its hopeful efforts produce institution-sustaining fruit, the more its borderline comic/romantic tone may shift toward the less optimistic alternatives. Or, on the other side, a church with an ironic tone might only need the encouragement of a few fruitful ministry projects to move toward a more romantic tone.

Early Childhood and Imagery

In early childhood, our minds are like sponges in that storying is largely spent collecting imagery with little notion of discernment or consistency. McAdams notes, "Children are not in a position to determine the quality of the imagery to which they are exposed."[3] With regard to storied faith development, his qualification suggests that some individuals will absorb stories rapidly whether those stories are helpful or healthy or not. There is a need, if the church's story is to be carefully discerned, for these individuals to learn how to be more selective of the stories they receive by thinking critically about their media consumption and its messaging. For a congregation in the early childhood stage, attention must be paid to the dominant language and imagery being used and the primary metaphors the church has for understanding itself. How are we talking about God and our participation in the mission of God?

This attentiveness to imagery and metaphor is crucial inasmuch as those things reflect the theological models by which a church operates. Every congregation is guided by models and metaphors that "often determine how we feel about ourselves and our world, and how we conduct ourselves in it," so we would do well to be aware of the prevailing metaphors and models in the church if we are to monitor their influence upon us.[4] Story-centered renewal implores a congregation to be aware of which are the more resonant metaphors. This discovery and discernment of central metaphor was the intent of the summer sermon series on biblical metaphor (see figure 5.2) mentioned in chapter 5. PUCC had been straddling the line between the early childhood stage and the next stage, and that exercise helped move the congregation forward in its development.

Late Childhood and Narrative Theme

In the late childhood stage, we begin to understand narrative themes, foremost of which are power and love. McAdams defines narrative theme as "a recurrent pattern of human intention. It is the level of story concerned with what the characters in the narrative want and how they pursue their objectives over time."[5] A story's theme answers the question, "Why?" Why does Raskolnikov confess to his crime? Why do the man and boy persevere on their painstaking journey down *The Road*? Why does Jonas reject his role as the Receiver of Memory and flee his utopian community? Why does Dr. Rieux continue to treat plague victims despite his sense of futility?

In terms of the church story, it is the question of mission and purpose with regard to praxis: "Why does the church do what it does?" As noted in chapter 1, Diana Butler Bass suggests this is a missing piece in the life of many churches. Many churches suffer for prescribing or expecting certain practices without connecting them to a narrative theme.[6] To ensure the church's story ends up being congruent, we must learn to recognize and think in terms of narrative themes and answering the "Why?" questions.

Likewise, a congregation in late childhood must begin to identify the narrative themes of its story. What are the values and motivations behind its ministry? Typically, the narrative themes emerge in connection to the resonant metaphors identified in early childhood. For instance, once PUCC had identified family and table as central metaphors to its church life, narrative themes of strengthening relationship and offering hospitality emerged as predominant answers to the "Why?" of ministry decisions.

Adolescence and Identity

In adolescence, the story finally becomes a more articulate expression of our personal identity as it occurs in dialogue with the world of which we understand ourselves to be a part. Because of that collaborative dynamic, it is necessary in the storied development process to raise both an individual and communal awareness of the world and the church's ministry context. As noted in chapter 1, demographic tools such as MissionInsite are invaluable in the effort to understand the macrocommunity.

Once it is aware of its situatedness, a church can acknowledge that any change to its situation is likely to impact the story. As a result, adolescence—as actual teenage adolescence tends to be—is a stage often marked by dramatic shifts between floundering uncertainty and confident creativity. Some days we sure of who we are, and other days we feel totally lost. In fact, McAdams describes story-making as a pendulum process, saying, "We should expect alternating and irregular phases of exploration and commitment. . . . During periods of exploration, the person is likely to be revising [the story]. During periods of commitment, [the story] remains relatively stable."[7] Churches, like people, can swing from one season to another.

No days are more difficult or make the fragility of identity more evident than when we are faced with change. However, I am convinced that the uncomfortable liminal spaces created by changes like pastoral leadership transitions, major church decisions, or unforeseen challenges like the coronavirus are ideal occasions for taking a long, hard look at the congregation's story. In many instances, we occupy those liminal spaces because the situation has changed, and so the story and its embodiment must be revised. We must reach a renewed understanding of our context in order to tell a story authentic to its renewed identity, but that renewal necessitates coming to a better understanding of the world in which the church now exists. Adolescence can be an awkward stage, even painful at times, but also a stage with room for profound growth.

Young Adulthood and the Imago

The dynamism of story continues in the young adulthood stage, during which we refine our sense of who we are in our story. McAdams uses the term *imago* to refer to the personification of our most treasured traits and our espoused values. However, he acknowledges that individuals usually hold multiple imagoes in tension because "our lives are generally too complex to be populated by a single main character."[8] For instance, I can think of myself as a father, a son, a pastor, a writer, and so forth, and all will be true but none single-handedly captures who I am. A similar complexity occurs in the church story, since it is always the product of a community of individuals, each with their own story, and because even if a church centers its story on one or a few resonant metaphors, none will ever completely capture its fullness.

For instance, the church that likes to consider itself a friendly church will tell stories in which it exhibits this friendliness. Yet ministry and congregational life are too complex and "friendliness" too subjective a term to be the only trait of a church imago. Or while PUCC may resonate most closely with metaphors of family and table and themes emerging from them, it must be aware of ways in which other metaphors and themes also show up in congregational life and ministry. While refuge or tabernacle may not be primary to the church's story, members of the congregation and community may have attitudes about worship containing traces of escapism and exclusivism. While the church may not see itself as a fortress of faith under attack, it must be cognizant of the persecution complex of American Christianity and its potential influence on conversations about mission. It is imperative that churches understand the dynamism of a story that is polyphonic and, if not constantly being revised, doomed to devolve into generality and irrelevance.

Middle Adulthood and Resolution

Despite the dynamism and multiplicity inherent in story, individuals and communities trend toward convergence: "Ultimately, we seek unity as much as diversity. We seek to be one thing, for the story, no matter how complex, must still be the single story for a single life," and for a single congregation.[9] This is why, in middle adulthood, people work toward resolution in the story. Where there are imagoes that contradict, the instinct is to wrestle with how central or strong those vying values are and to determine whether compromise is possible or whether one must be chosen over the other. The most enduring ones will be those that "blend agency and communion."[10] Every metaphor and combination of metaphors used to formulate a story carries with it sticking points. This stage involves acknowledging the challenges and confronting them. It means establishing healthy ways for conflict and disagreement to be voiced and mediated so that it is neither ignored nor destructive to the community. It means every story-centered church must be willing to navigate tension with a commitment to enduring unity.

For instance, let us consider the potential tension that can arise within PUCC's family-table metaphors. One of the challenges of the family metaphor is the struggle to maintain peacefulness among the members. Families can be very close knit, but fighting among family members is often the bitterest fighting you will find. One of the challenges of the table metaphor is the underlying fear of losing one's place—one's seat. Therefore, one of the challenges for a family-table church like PUCC is when communal life becomes something like the awkward Thanksgiving dinner where no one wants to mention divisive topics for fear of disturbing the illusion of peace and unity and possibly being dismissed. The middle adulthood stage responds to the tension of those challenges by finding healthy ways to resolve them rather than avoid them.

Late Adulthood and Legacy

Finally, late adulthood is when we create legacy stories to pass on to the next generation. While I have dealt in chapter 2 with the generative nature of the Christian story, here it is worth mentioning several characteristics of highly generative individuals that I believe parallel the characteristics of a highly generative church. Generative people possess a sense of chosenness and calling, an unwavering conviction of purpose, and firsthand examples of redemption in their lives.[11] Likewise, a generative church should possess a strong sense of identity, of mission, and of having been transformed by God.

Ideally, the storied church becomes a highly generative church as a result of its development. To each subsequent generation of the church's life is bequeathed a clearer sense of communal story, a more honest and humble congregational culture that is open and attentive to revising the story when necessary, and the practical ministry tools for doing that revision work.

Questions for Reflection

- Into which storied developmental stage does your church seem to fit organizationally?

- Into which stage of storied faith development would you say most individuals in your church fall?

- How will recognizing or naming your organization's stage of storied development help you address issues and become more generative?

Notes

Preface: A Brief Story on Writing This Book

1   Jonathan Gottschall, *The Storytelling Animal: How Stories Make Us Human*, read by Kris Koscheski (New York: Houghton Mifflin Harcourt, 2012), audiobook.

Chapter 1: Church in Search of Story

1   Diana Butler Bass, *Christianity for the Rest of Us: How the Neighborhood Church Is Transforming the Faith* (San Francisco: HarperOne, 2006), 38.

2   Bass, 282.

3   Norman L. Jones, "Calvinistic Character of the Early German Reformed Church," RCUS, April 4, 2009, http://www.rcus.org/calvinistic-character/.

4   Jones.

5   James I. Good, "The German Reformed Church in Colonial America," RCUS, April 4, 2009, http://www.rcus.org/reformed-colonial/.

6   Statistics based on a MissionInsite report surveying area within a three-mile radius of PUCC. In actuality, the area includes portions of adjacent towns but is a more accurate representation of the church's macro-community. "Custom Demographics Report," MissionInsite, accessed September 1, 2018, https://peopleview.missioninsite.com/app/#/welcome/demographics/step-5. MissionInsite is an invaluable surveying tool for gathering data on your local community. I highly recommend using it to understand the trends in your community because the data it provides will tell you a story about what is happening around you.

7   Ray Oldenburg, *The Great Good Place: Cafes, Coffee Shops, Bookstores, Bars, Hair Salons and Other Hangouts at the Heart of a Community*, 10th anniversary ed. (Cambridge, MA: Da Capo, 1999).

8   Peter Block, *Community: The Structure of Belonging* (San Francisco: Berrett-Koehler, 2009), 5.

9   Stephen C. Compton, *Rekindling the Mainline: New Life through New Churches* (Bethesda, MD: Alban Institute, 2003), 6.

10   Compton, 6.

11   Linda Bergquist and Allan Karr, *Church Turned Inside Out: A Guide for Designers, Refiners, and Re-aligners* (San Francisco: Jossey-Bass, 2010), 139. Bergquist and Karr employ the term *legacy church*, which I am treating here as synonymous with the definition of *village church* that I have presented.

12   Joel Coen and Ethan Coen, dirs., *The Big Lebowski* (Universal City, CA: Gramercy Pictures, 1998), DVD (Universal City, CA: Universal Studios, 2003).

13   Søren Kierkegaard, "The Sickness unto Death," in *A Kierkegaard Anthology*, ed. Robert Bretall (Princeton, NJ: Princeton University Press, 1973). In his existential treatise, Kierkegaard describes despair as a separation from both God and self. At an institutional level, that defines the despair of so many mainline congregations.

14   Stephen Crites, "The Narrative Quality of Experience" (1971), in *Why Narrative? Readings in Narrative Theology*, ed. Stanley Hauerwas and L. Gregory Jones (Eugene, OR: Wipf & Stock, 1997). While I will give him a more thorough introduction in the next section, Crites describes here the effect wherein experience itself feels adversarial, and our instinct is to either rationalize the discomfort or cover it up because either one feels easier than finding a new story. That instinct, rather than providing resolution, actually compounds the despair: "Experience becomes demonically possessed by its own abstracting and contracting possibilities, turned alien and hostile to experience itself. When the humanities give up the story, they become alternately seized by desiccated abstractions and scatological immediacies, the light of the mind becoming a blinding and withering glare, the friendly darkness deepening into the chaotic night of nihilism" (86–87).

15   Kierkegaard, "Sickness unto Death," 351.

16   Bass, *Christianity for the Rest of Us*, 223. These characteristics of "nomadic existence" closely parallel the characteristics of isolation, impermanence, and historical discontinuity.

17   Bass, 243.

18   Diana Butler Bass, *Christianity after Religion: The End of Church and the Birth of a New Spiritual Awakening* (San Francisco: HarperOne, 2012), 183.

19   Bass, 237 (emphasis mine).

20   Dan P. McAdams, *The Stories We Live By: Personal Myths and the Making of the Self* (New York: William Morrow, 1993), 30. While his word choice *actors* has connotations that could suggest duplicity, I understand McAdams here to be simply indicating human agency.

21   Paul Ricoeur, *Time and Narrative*, trans. Kathleen McLaughlin and David Pellauer (Chicago: University of Chicago, 1984), 1:x.

22   Ricoeur, 1:xi.

23   McAdams, *Stories We Live By*, 102.

24   McAdams, 227.

25   Ricoeur, *Time and Narrative*, 1:19. See also Rex Warner, trans., *The Confessions of Saint Augustine*, bk. 11, chap. 20 (New York: Signet Classic, 2001), 268.

26   Ricoeur, *Time and Narrative*, 1:52.

27   Bergquist and Karr lament this characteristic of legacy/village churches, who "connect the past and the present, and though they are positioned well to address the future most have not yet imagined how their model could be uniquely positioned to transform their changing macrocommunity." Bergquist and Karr, *Church Turned Inside Out*, 138.

28   The use of Story as a proper noun is to differentiate between the various kinds of stories we tell as humans bound by time and the divine narrative behind and over all existence. I will write in chapter 2 about the subjectivity of deciding what we believe the Story to be about, but here it is only necessary to note that the church's story bears a sense of both humility and empowerment in its connectivity to the will and work of God. Because I'm specifically writing about churches and not secular institutions, I am assuming the larger Story will be that of God's redemptive plan for creation. However, McAdams allows that the overarching Story need not be understood as theistic: "The stories we live by are enhanced by our faith and our fidelity to something larger and nobler than the self—be that something God, the human spirit, progress through technology, or some other transcendent end." McAdams, *Stories We Live By*, 174.

29   This is in contrast to the unpleasant alternative Ricoeur describes: "The soul, deprived of the stillness of the eternal present, is torn asunder." Ricoeur, *Time and Narrative*, 1:27.

30   Ricoeur, 1:33.

31   Crites, "Narrative Quality of Experience," 70.

32   Crites, 71.

33   Crites, 71.

34   Crites, 68.

35   Sallie McFague TeSelle, *Speaking in Parables: A Study in Metaphor and Theology* (Philadelphia: Fortress, 1975), 1.

Chapter 2: A Storied Faith

1   I begin the chapter this way because I agree with Walter Brueggemann: "These exchanges are the starting point for the literary, canonical process, as well as for the educational process. . . . They are aimed at worship, but worship as pedagogy, the engagement of the young in the normative claims of the community." From Walter Brueggemann, *The Creative Word: Canon as a Model for Biblical Education*, 2nd ed. (Minneapolis: Fortress, 2015), 20. The probable exilic context of such a conversation is wonderfully reimagined in Sean Gladding's *The Story of God, the Story of Us* (Downers Grove, IL: InterVarsity, 2010).

2   Brueggemann, *Creative Word*, 31.

3   McFague TeSelle, *Speaking in Parables*, 1–2.

4   James Cone, *God of the Oppressed*, rev. ed. (Maryknoll, NY: Orbis, 1997), 93 (emphasis mine).

5   In *Speaking in Parables*, McFague TeSelle repeatedly stresses metaphor, parable, and story as vehicles for process and movement: "We *move*, through metaphor, to meaning; metaphor is a *motion* from here to there" (32); "Metaphoric meaning is a *process*, not a momentary, static insight; it operates like a story, moving from here to there, from 'what is' to 'what might be'" (33); "Metaphor is movement, human movement; without it, we would not be what we are. . . . The process is a dialectic of imagining new frames and contexts for our ordinary worlds, of seeing a new world which is also the old world" (58).

6   Annette Simmons, *Whoever Tells the Best Story Wins: How to Use Your Own Stories to Communicate with Power and Impact*, 2nd ed. (New York: Amacom, 2015), 13–14.

7   Cone, *God of the Oppressed*, 95.

8   John Navone cites John Drury's idea of the human appetite for stories: "We do not live by bread alone, but by every word that proceeds from the mouth of God. Our appetite for stories derives from the Creator. As storylistening and storytelling animals, we have a created appetite for God's words, for the stories that he tells in the lives of others. It is an appetite for news from elsewhere which shows us our way about in the here and now, a conjunction of the strange and the

familiar." John Navone, *Towards a Theology of Story* (Slough: St. Paul, 1977), 21.

9   Wolfgang Petersen, dir., *The NeverEnding Story* (Burbank, CA: Warner Brothers, 1984), DVD (Burbank, CA: Warner Brothers, 2001). For another similarly illustrative metaphor, see Evan Turk's children's story *The Storyteller* (New York: Atheneum Books for Young Readers, 2016). It describes a desert village being saved from a sandstorm when the villagers conjure water through the telling of stories.

10   Norbert Haukenfrers, *Fire, Water, and Wind: God's Transformational Narrative: Learning from Narrative Psychology, Neuroscience, and Storytelling about Identity Formation* (Eugene, OR: Wipf & Stock, 2016), 50.

11   Haukenfrers, 26.

12   The contrast here is paraphrased from a similar one used by John Dominic Crossan: "The classical mind says, that's only a story, but the modern mind says, there's only story." John Dominic Crossan, *The Dark Interval: Towards a Theology of Story* (Sonoma, CA: Polebridge, 1988), 29.

13   Leonard Sweet, foreword to Haukenfrers, *Fire, Water, and Wind*, xi.

14   David L. Barr, *New Testament Story: An Introduction*, 3rd ed. (Belmont, CA: Wadsworth-Thomson Learning, 2002), 5.

15   Brueggemann, *Creative Word*, 9.

16   "A living tradition then is an historically extended, socially embodied argument, and an argument precisely in part about the goods which constitute that tradition." Alasdair MacIntyre, "Virtues, Unity of a Human Life, and Tradition," in Hauerwas and Jones, *Why Narrative?*, 107. In other words, "living" implies that rather than being fixed or static, tradition has set the trajectory for present practice while remaining malleable.

17   Sallie McFague, *Metaphorical Theology: Models of God in Religious Language* (Philadelphia: Fortress, 1982), 3.

18   McFague, 56.

19   MacIntyre uses a brilliant example of Galileo's impact on the scientific tradition. The line I'm paraphrasing here reads, "It introduces new standards for evaluating the past. It recasts the narrative which constitutes the continuous reconstruction of the scientific tradition." Alasdair MacIntyre, "Epistemological Crises, Narrative, and Philosophy of Science," in Hauerwas and Jones, *Why Narrative?*, 146.

20   McFague TeSelle, *Speaking in Parables*, 23.

21   "God of Grace and God of Glory," by Harry Emerson Fosdick, 1930.

22   McFague, *Metaphorical Theology*, 14.

23   Navone, *Towards a Theology of Story*, 26.

24   Brueggemann, *Creative Word*, 31.

25   "Israel does not propose to offer a story which is true for everyone all the time." Brueggemann, 38.

26   Amy Erickson, foreword to Brueggemann, *Creative Word*, x.

27   "This means that we cannot say our metaphors 'correspond' to 'what is'; at best, we can only say that they seem appropriate to our experience, they 'fit' or seem 'right.'" McFague TeSelle, *Speaking in Parables*, 51.

28   Brueggemann, *Creative Word*, 33.

29   One could argue, as Rick Sessoms does, that literacy and the printed word have been as much a blessing to the pursuit and sharing of information as they are a detriment to the storying imagination. Rick Sessoms with Tim Brannagan, *Leading with Story: Cultivating Christ-Centered Leaders in a Storycentric Generation* (Pasadena, CA: William Carey Library, 2016), 19.

30   Wilda C. Gafney, *The Womanist Midrash: A Reintroduction to the Women of the Torah and the Throne* (Louisville: Westminster John Knox, 2017), 4.

31   Johann Baptist Metz, "A Short Apology of Narrative," trans. David Smith, in Hauerwas and Jones, *Why Narrative?*, 255.

32   "In most places and times, the fairy tale has not been specially made for, nor exclusively enjoyed by, children. It has gravitated to the nursery when it became unfashionable in literary circles." C. S. Lewis, *On Stories: And Other Essays on Literature* (New York: Harcourt, 1982), 35.

33   Lewis, 33.

34   Lewis, 38.

35   MacIntyre, "Virtues," 101–2.

36   Lewis, *On Stories*, 39.

37   Sessoms cites a 2003 National Assessment of Adult Literacy study and suggests that 80 percent of the world's people and 70 percent of Americans could be considered story-centric learners. Sessoms with Brannagan, *Leading with Story*, xxi.

38   Lewis, *On Stories*, 47.

39   Lewis, 48.

40   Stephen King, It (New York: Signet, 1980), 855.

41   Metz, "Short Apology of Narrative," 252.

42   Metz, 252.

43   Cone, *God of the Oppressed*, 94.

44   See Brueggemann's discussion of the Solomonic kingdom in Walter
      Brueggemann, *The Prophetic Imagination* (Philadelphia: Fortress,
      1978), 32–37.

45   Brueggemann, *Creative Word*, 82.

46   Rage Against the Machine, "Testify," on *The Battle of Los Angeles*,
      recorded 1999, Epic Records.

47   "Prose is always the language of the king, of the 'managerial men-
      tality.' If the prophet can be reduced to prose, then the message can
      be translated into a program. And the program, predictably, will be
      administered by the same people who administer everything else."
      Brueggemann, *Creative Word*, 74–75. It is important to understand
      that Brueggemann here is defining *poetic* and *prosaic* in an Aristo-
      telian fashion. It is not a distinction between two literary genres
      but rather a dichotomy between one that is literary and one that
      is decidedly not. Therefore, despite the synonymous way in which
      we use the terms *story* and *prose* today, in this dichotomy and in my
      understanding of its nature and function, story is poetry, not prose.

48   One might counter here by noting the centrality of the Davidic king-
      dom to Hebrew Scripture and postexilic Judaism. I suggest that the
      story of Esther along with the prophetic yearning for Emmanuel
      (God with us) are indicative that even the Davidic legacy is meant to
      be a cautionary tale illustrating the flaw of exchanging trust in God
      for trust in fallible human leadership. See also the prophet's warning
      in 1 Sam 8.

49   Cone, *God of the Oppressed*, 94.

50   Brueggemann asserts, "Persons who are nurtured into irony, meta-
      phor, and parable are persons who are likely to maintain some crit-
      ical distance from every managed world." Brueggemann, *Creative
      Word*, 75.

51   Brueggemann places particular emphasis on overcoming the numb-
      ness surrounding death in chapter 3 of *Prophetic Imagination*. More
      recently, funeral director Caleb Wilde has written in favor of a
      "death-positive" view in his *Confessions of a Funeral Director: How
      the Business of Death Saved My Life* (New York: HarperOne, 2017).

52   Brueggemann, *Creative Word*, 77.

53   "No prophet ever sees things under the aspect of eternity. It is always
      partisan theology, always for the moment, always for the concrete
      community." Brueggemann, *Prophetic Imagination*, 24.

54   Brueggemann, *Creative Word*, 71–72.

55   Brueggemann, 73–74.

56   Rachel Held Evans, *Inspired: Slaying Giants, Walking on Water, and Loving the Bible Again* (Nashville: Nelson, 2018), 162. The book is an accessible exploration of the various genres of story found in the Bible.

57   Crossan, *Dark Interval*, 42.

58   McFague TeSelle, *Speaking in Parables*, 78.

59   For clarification, Crossan locates "myth" and "parable" on opposite ends of a story-type spectrum. Between them are "satire," "apologue," and "action." The juxtaposition that Crossan notes between myth and parable is that myths establish and sustain the world (and often the status quo), while parables are told, within the language and context of those myths, in order to subvert that world. Crossan, *Dark Interval*, 42–44.

60   Crossan, 82.

61   "The tradition of the primitive church changed these stories from parables into moral examples or exemplary stories and/or historical allegories. . . . In effecting this change the early church moved these stories back into literary types well-known from the carefully constructed pedagogical methods of the rabbis." Crossan, 101.

62   McFague TeSelle, *Speaking in Parables*, 69 (emphasis hers).

63   John Dominic Crossan, *The Power of Parable: How Fiction by Jesus Became Fiction about Jesus* (San Francisco: HarperOne, 2012), 102. I don't think Crossan's use of the word *primitive* is meant to be pejorative; rather, it refers to the earliest manifestations of the Christian church.

64   Evans, *Inspired*, 151.

65   McFague TeSelle, *Speaking in Parables*, 82 (emphasis hers).

66   "For the Christian, the story of Jesus is the story par excellence. For his story not only is the human struggle of moving toward belief but in some way that story is the unification of the mundane and the transcendent." McFague TeSelle, 139.

67   McFague TeSelle, 94.

68   "What must always be kept in mind is that the parables as metaphors and the life of Jesus as a metaphor of God provide characteristics for theology: a theology guided by them is open-ended, tentative, indirect, tensive, iconoclastic, transformative." McFague, *Metaphorical Theology*, 19.

69   Niebuhr, "Story of Our Life," 44.

Chapter 3: A Storied Community

1   John Hughes, dir., *The Breakfast Club* (Universal City, CA: Universal Pictures, 1985), DVD (Universal City, CA: Universal Pictures, 2008).

2   Dietrich Bonhoeffer, *Life Together*, trans. John W. Doberstein (New York: Harper & Row, 1976), 30.

3   Stephen Denning makes a similar note with respect to organizational/business culture: "Culture is transmitted not in formal doctrines or official processes but mainly through stories—anecdotes, jokes, epigrams, or proverbs." Stephen Denning, *The Leader's Guide to Storytelling: Mastering the Art and Discipline of Business Narrative*, 2nd ed. (San Francisco: Jossey-Bass, 2011), 208–9.

4   Bruxy Cavey, *The End of Religion: Encountering the Subversive Spirituality of Jesus* (Toronto: Agora Imprints, 2005), 66.

5   Thomas Porter, *The Spirit and Art of Conflict Transformation: Creating a Culture of Just Peace* (Nashville: Upper Room, 2010), 41.

6   Kenneth Cloke and Joan Goldsmith, *Resolving Personal and Organizational Conflict: Stories of Transformation and Forgiveness* (San Francisco: Jossey-Bass, 2000), 5.

7   Cloke and Goldsmith, 58.

8   Porter, *Spirit and Art*, 45.

9   Bill W., *Twelve Steps and Twelve Traditions* (New York: Alcoholics Anonymous World Services, 1984), 16.

10   George H. Jensen traces the history and influence of temperance groups like the Washingtonians, which became infatuated with public spectacle, and the Oxford Group, which held an explicitly Christian worldview. Knowing its roots and how these influencing organizations were undermined by certain characteristics helps one appreciate why the founders of Alcoholics Anonymous were so adamant about its nonsectarian status. George H. Jensen, *Storytelling in Alcoholics Anonymous: A Rhetorical Analysis* (Carbondale: Southern Illinois University Press, 2000), 15–32.

11   Keith Humphreys, "Community Narratives and Personal Stories in Alcoholics Anonymous," *Journal of Community Psychology* 28, no. 5 (2000): 496.

12   Humphreys, 505.

13   In the following section, I will attend briefly to the ways in which the Twelve Steps contribute to postures of humility and honesty, but I will attribute those as much to the practice of storytelling as to the spiritual content of the Steps. For those interested in a deeper exploration of the spiritual connections, Richard Rohr has written

an excellent book on the topic. Richard Rohr, *Breathing under Water: Spirituality and the Twelve Steps* (Cincinnati: Franciscan Media, 2011).

14   This is a brief paraphrase of Tradition One. W., *Twelve Steps and Twelve Traditions*, 130.

15   Tradition Two notes that leaders are expected to be servants, not superiors or authorities. W., 132.

16   W., 139.

17   Tradition Five reflects a notably evangelical, rather than institutional, mindset. W., 150.

18   Traditions Six and Ten, especially, as well as Tradition Eight to a degree.

19   Tradition Eleven. W., *Twelve Steps and Twelve Traditions*, 180.

20   Jensen, *Storytelling in Alcoholics Anonymous*, ix.

21   Jensen, 11.

22   Humphreys, "Community Narratives and Personal Stories," 499.

23   Humphreys, 500.

24   Jensen, *Storytelling in Alcoholics Anonymous*, 77.

25   "To speak about one's story within the culture of an AA meeting is to live the tradition and culture of the organization. . . . As the speaker learns to speak as the others in that community speak, he or she shares a new identity." Jensen, 112. Note how closely this language resembles that of the living storied faith tradition discussed in chapter 2.

26   "The purpose of relating drunk-a-logs to potential AA members is to get listeners to see commonalities between their own experience and that of the speaker." Humphreys, "Community Narratives and Personal Stories," 500.

27   Humphreys, 501.

28   Jensen, *Storytelling in Alcoholics Anonymous*, 48.

29   Humphreys, "Community Narratives and Personal Stories," 502.

30   Humphreys, 503.

31   Humphreys, 504.

32   Jensen, *Storytelling in Alcoholics Anonymous*, 93.

33   Rohr, *Breathing under Water*, 123.

34   Bonhoeffer, *Life Together*, 110.

35   W., *Twelve Steps and Twelve Traditions*, 42.

36   W., 55.

37   Bonhoeffer, *Life Together*, 119.

38   W., *Twelve Steps and Twelve Traditions*, 57.

39   Rohr, *Breathing under Water*, 43.

40   "The steps, thus, inform much of the structure—and, one might add, content—of AA stories. Further, it is by working the steps that one develops a 'voice' that is unique yet clearly situated within the ethos of the program." Jensen, *Storytelling in Alcoholics Anonymous*, 51.

41   Jensen, 80.

42   Jensen, 94.

43   Jensen, 109.

44   Rohr, *Breathing under Water*, 45–46.

45   Rohr quips, "AA is the only group I know that is willing and honest enough to just tell people up front, 'You are damn selfish!' Or, 'Until you get beyond your massive narcissism you are never going to grow up.'" Rohr, 71.

46   W., *Twelve Steps and Twelve Traditions*, 45–46.

47   W., 91.

48   "Confession as a routine duty is spiritual death; confession as reliance upon the promise is life." Bonhoeffer, *Life Together*, 120.

49   Navone, *Towards a Theology of Story*, 74.

50   Navone, 75. Haukenfrers goes a step further by suggesting, "We cannot assume that we are living a storied life unless we are witnessing change in our life and change around us." Haukenfrers, *Fire, Water, and Wind*, 68.

51   Leonard Sweet, foreword to Haukenfrers, *Fire, Water, and Wind*, xi.

Chapter 4: Finding a Story amid the Stories

1   Stephen King, *The Gunslinger: The Dark Tower I*, rev. and expanded ed. (New York: Signet, 2003), 266.

2   Annette Simmons, *The Story Factor: Inspiration, Influence, and Persuasion through the Art of Storytelling*, rev. ed. (New York: Basic Books, 2006), 224.

3   Simmons, 225.

4   McAdams, *Stories We Live By*, 174.

5   Simmons, *Whoever Tells the Best Story*, 2.

6   Stephen King, *On Writing: A Memoir on the Craft*, 10th anniversary ed. (New York: Scribner, 2010).

7   Thomas Groome, *Christian Religious Education: Sharing Our Story and Vision* (San Francisco: Jossey-Bass, 1999), 184.

8   Groome, 192.

9   Groome, 194.

10   Julie Anne Lytle, "Moving Online: Faith Formation in a Digital Age," *Lifelong Faith Journal* 4, no. 1 (Spring 2010): 41.

11   McAdams, *Stories We Live By*, 126.

12   Godin, *All Marketers Are Liars*, 160.

13   Godin, 161.

14   Godin, 159.

15   "Beginning around 1890, denominations built massive bureaucratic structures, modeling themselves after American businesses, complete with corporate headquarters, program divisions, professional development and marketing departments, franchises (parish churches), training centers, and career tracks. Other than the fact that denominations offered religion as the product, they differed little from other corporations that dominated America in the last century." Bass, *Christianity after Religion*, 71–72.

16   Salmon, *Storytelling: Bewitching the Modern Mind*, trans. David Macey (New York: Verso, 2010), 24.

17   Godin, *All Marketers Are Liars*, 150.

18   McAdams, *Stories We Live By*, 12.

19   Simmons, *Whoever Tells the Best Story*, 11.

20   Carol Howard Merritt has written a poignant essay on narrative in the social media age in which she contrasts the polished pews against the dusty chairs of AA meetings: "Pastors see the shiny backs of those empty pews on Sunday morning and realize that something just as profound was happening in the twelve-step meetings in the basement while we were upstairs in the pretty sanctuary. In those groups, they were not dusting themselves off to show their newness: people were sharing their broken selves. They were presenting their shattered lives in order to form a different sort of community." Carol Howard Merritt, "Net-A-Narratives: The Evolution of the Story in Our Culture," in *The Hyphenateds: How Emergence Christianity Is Re-traditioning Mainline Practices*, ed. Phil Snider (St. Louis: Chalice, 2011), 67.

21   Annette Simmons argues for the superiority of authentic stories even at an aesthetic level: "Stories that are cleaned up are not as interesting as untidy, but more human, stories." Simmons, *Whoever Tells the Best Story*, 184.

22   Denning, *Leader's Guide to Storytelling*, 67–68.

23   Denning, 123.

24   Denning, 280.

25   Salmon, *Storytelling*, 100.

26   Salmon, 99.

27 "The credibility of the narrator is therefore the key to a narrative's performativity." Salmon, 146.

28 Godin, *All Marketers Are Liars*, 20.

29 Stanley Hauerwas and L. Gregory Jones, eds., "Introduction: Why Narrative?," in Hauerwas and Jones, *Why Narrative?*, 10.

30 Denning, *Leader's Guide to Storytelling*, 266.

31 Godin, *All Marketers Are Liars*, 89.

32 Denning, *Leader's Guide to Storytelling*, 109–10.

33 Salmon, *Storytelling*, 16.

34 Simmons, *Whoever Tells the Best Story*, 177.

35 Simmons, 167.

36 Simmons, *Story Factor*, 85.

37 Denning, *Leader's Guide to Storytelling*, 136.

38 Denning, 158.

39 Denning, 214.

40 "If there is some sense that 'who you are' isn't who you say you are, then you have other issues to fix before you tell your story. True faith in your organization is based in honesty." Simmons, *Whoever Tells the Best Story*, 168.

41 Salmon, *Storytelling*, 39.

42 Godin, *All Marketers Are Liars*, 98.

Chapter 5: Integrating Story Centrality

1 So far as I am aware, Christian educator James F. Hopewell was one of the first people to suggest that the search for storied self could be applied at the local church level. He posited that since the church is an innately human institution, personal developmental processes can also be observed communally. James F. Hopewell, *Congregation: Stories and Structures* (Philadelphia: Fortress, 1987).

2 Herbert Anderson and Edward Foley, *Mighty Stories, Dangerous Rituals: Weaving Together the Human and the Divine* (San Francisco: Jossey-Bass, 1998), 18.

3 Including the influence of James W. Fowler, who notably based his study of the stages of faith development on Erikson's model and, so doing, is a natural conversation partner with McAdams and the storiedness of faith. James W. Fowler, *Stages of Faith: The Psychology of Human Development and the Quest for Meaning* (San Francisco: HarperCollins, 1981).

4   Jane Rogers Vann, *Gathered before God: Worship-Centered Church Renewal* (Louisville: Westminster John Knox, 2004), 33.

5   Vann, 26.

6   Anderson and Foley, *Mighty Stories*, ix.

7   Anderson and Foley, 27.

8   "Often the untold stories are the ones with the most power." Anderson and Foley, 79.

9   Anderson and Foley, 40–41.

10   Anderson and Foley, 164.

11   "Our impulse to tell the story of God in our communities is the right one, but making speeches is the wrong way to do it." Doug Pagitt, *Preaching in the Inventive Age* (Nashville: Abingdon, 2014), 13.

12   Many years prior to Pagitt, renowned preacher Fred Craddock had already begun wrestling with the growing inadequacy of the traditional sermon in an increasingly post-Christian American society. He had noticed something was lacking—that there was an "illusion of participation [in the Christian faith] where little or none actually exists." Fred Craddock, *Overhearing the Gospel: Preaching and Teaching the Faith to Persons Who Have Heard It All Before* (Nashville: Abingdon, 1978), 24.

13   Craddock makes the case that this shift from formation to information can be attributed at least in part to the modern rise of historical biblical criticism and its obsession with facticity, which helped dehumanize the storied faith (73–74). Further, he writes,

> What has happened is that under the rubric of historical criticism the Tradition [read "storied faith"] has been turned into history. The Tradition is a narrative, an ingenious mingling of history and non-history, experience and interpretation, into a continuous story. Because that story is alive, modifying and being modified by the terrain of generations through which it passes, including the present, then it is my story. History, on the other hand, was; it happened and has been recorded, and hence is not my story but theirs. Only by a diligent hermeneutical endeavor can it be brought into my world. In the Tradition narrative we are participants in the sequence, not independent observers. A Tradition renders its meaning and power to the community and to its individual members by the very process of narration which is indispensible to the Tradition. (75)

14   Not coincidentally, in viewing "speaching" to be a symptom of the professionalization of ministry, the presentation of progressional

dialogue is reminiscent of AA's Tradition Eight, forbidding the professionalization of its leadership.

15   It is worth noting that Pagitt also delves into the impact that the use of a pulpit and sound system have on conveying authority and power implicitly.

16   "When the content of the sermon is created in the isolated setting of the pastor's mind and study and is delivered to whomever happens to be at church that Sunday, it has all the impact of a bumper sticker." Pagitt, *Preaching in the Inventive Age*, 80.

17   Anderson and Foley, *Mighty Stories*, 44.

18   Craddock, *Overhearing the Gospel*, 80. The reason I spent chapter 3 discussing the characteristics of storied community is due to the reasonable question here of whether persons would view their church community as one that is loving and trustworthy. If not, participation in progressional dialogue will suffer. A church in the Infancy stage of its storied development may struggle to incorporate progressional dialogue.

19   For this specific combination of core metaphors, the church looked on a book by Leonard Sweet that was profoundly insightful in imagining the implications of a ministry shaped by its core metaphors. Leonard Sweet, *From Tablet to Table: Where Community Is Found and Identity Is Formed* (Colorado Springs: NavPress, 2014).

20   Celeste Kennel-Shank, "At Gilead Church in Chicago, Storytelling Is Central to Worship," *Christian Century*, April 24, 2019, https://tinyurl.com/4e8h5rbt.

21   Lillian Daniel, *Tell It like It Is: Reclaiming the Practice of Testimony* (Herndon, VA: Alban Institute, 2006), 12.

22   Daniel, 112.

23   Daniel, 154–55.

24   Mary McClintock Fulkerson and Marcia W. Mount Shoop, *A Body Broken, a Body Betrayed: Race, Memory, and Eucharist in White-Dominated Churches* (Eugene, OR: Cascade, 2015), 69.

25   Anderson and Foley, *Mighty Stories*, 34.

26   Anderson and Foley, xiii–xiv.

27   Anderson and Foley, 162.

28   Vann, *Gathered before God*, 95.

29   Vann, 70.

30   McClintock Fulkerson and Mount Shoop, *Body Broken*, 54. The authors are primarily concerned with the racial subtext communicated by eucharistic practices in mostly white mainline churches that espouse a commitment to justice. Their book is required reading

for any mainline church seeking to make being "multiracial" part of its story.

31   Vann, *Gathered before God*, 105.

32   Doug Pagitt suggests this charge originates during the information age's emphasis on knowledge. Doug Pagitt, *Church in the Inventive Age* (Nashville: Abingdon, 2014), 21–24.

33   Anne E. Streaty Wimberly, *Soul Stories: African American Christian Education*, rev. ed. (Nashville: Abingdon, 2005), xi.

34   Wimberly is careful to clarify the prioritization of the everyday story: "By placing our stories up front, the intention is not to compromise the importance of the Christian faith story disclosed in the Bible. Rather, the intent is to acknowledge that Christian education leaders/teachers and participants already have an agenda when they come to Christian education. Our stories are the agenda we bring to our study of the Christian faith story in the Bible and our Christian faith heritage" (27). The delineation she is making is a hallmark of liberation theologians and the theologies of most marginalized people groups, which once again demonstrates that story-centered faith and storied communities are more prevalent among historically marginalized groups with a more story-centric ontological framework. In this case, Wimberly's "story-linking" process is rooted in the African American experience and the heritage of slave communities: "Our African American forebears in slavery were cognizant of the Bible as a storied document with which they could link their own stories, and from which they could find direction and hope in the hard trials and tribulations of their circumstances" (4).

35   Wimberly, 30.

36   Evans, *Inspired*. Also considered for this study were Rob Bell, *What Is the Bible? How an Ancient Library of Poems, Letters, and Stories Can Transform the Way You Think and Feel about Everything* (New York: HarperOne, 2017); and Gladding, *Story of God*.

37   Flannery O'Connor, *The Complete Stories* (New York: Farrar, Straus and Giroux, 1971). See also the recent exploration of Christian virtue through the lens of classic fiction: Karen Swallow Prior, *On Reading Well: Finding the Good Life through Great Books* (Grand Rapids, MI: Brazos, 2018).

38   Sweet, *From Tablet to Table*, 108.

39   Simmons, *Whoever Tells the Best Story*, 24–26.

40   Simmons, 96.

41   Block, *Community*, 152.

42   Sweet, *From Tablet to Table*, 104.

Appendix

1   Fowler, *Stages of Faith*. Not only does Fowler notably base his study of the stages of faith development on Erikson's model, but Fowler further influences our understanding of storied development through his assertion that faith development, while related to age and qualified in those terms, is not constricted by the timeline of aging. I suggest that, like faith development, an individual's story thinking capacity is unbound by age constraints.

2   Hopewell, *Congregation*, 69–72.

3   McAdams, *Stories We Live By*, 65.

4   McFague, *Metaphorical Theology*, 107.

5   McAdams, *Stories We Live By*, 67.

6   "To know why provides a sense of purpose to our actions. If we know why we engage in a particular activity, we experience deeper spiritual connection in our work." Bass, *Christianity after Religion*, 154.

7   McAdams, *Stories We Live By*, 95.

8   McAdams, 37.

9   McAdams, 122.

10   McAdams, 208.

11   McAdams, 247–48.

Bibliography

Anderson, Herbert, and Edward Foley. *Mighty Stories, Dangerous Rituals: Weaving Together the Human and the Divine.* Minneapolis: Fortress, 2019.

Barr, David L. *New Testament Story: An Introduction.* 3rd ed. Belmont, CA: Wadsworth-Thomson Learning Group, 2002.

Bass, Diana Butler. *Christianity after Religion: The End of Church and the Birth of a New Spiritual Awakening.* San Francisco: HarperOne, 2012.

———. *Christianity for the Rest of Us: How the Neighborhood Church Is Transforming the Faith.* San Francisco: HarperOne, 2006.

Bell, Rob. *What Is the Bible? How an Ancient Library of Poems, Letters, and Stories Can Transform the Way You Think and Feel about Everything.* San Francisco: HarperOne, 2017.

Bergquist, Linda, and Allan Karr. *Church Turned Inside Out: A Guide for Designers, Refiners, and Re-aligners.* San Francisco: Jossey-Bass, 2010.

Block, Peter. *Community: The Structure of Belonging.* San Francisco: Berrett-Koehler, 2009.

Bonhoeffer, Dietrich. *Life Together.* Translated by John W. Doberstein. New York: Harper & Row, 1976.

Brueggemann, Walter. *The Creative Word: Canon as a Model for Biblical Education.* 2nd ed. Revised by Amy Erickson. Minneapolis: Fortress, 2015.

———. *The Prophetic Imagination.* Philadelphia: Fortress, 1978.

Cavey, Bruxy. *The End of Religion: Encountering the Subversive Spirituality of Jesus.* Toronto: Agora Imprints, 2005.

Cloke, Kenneth, and Joan Goldsmith. *Resolving Personal and Organizational Conflict: Stories of Transformation and Forgiveness.* San Francisco: Jossey-Bass, 2000.

Coen, Joel, and Ethan Coen, dirs. *The Big Lebowski.* Universal City, CA: Gramercy Pictures, 1998. DVD. Universal City, CA: Universal Studios, 2003.

Compton, Stephen C. *Rekindling the Mainline: New Life through New Churches.* Bethesda, MD: Alban Institute, 2003.

Cone, James H. *God of the Oppressed.* 2nd ed. Maryknoll, NY: Orbis, 1997.

Craddock, Fred B. *Overhearing the Gospel: Preaching and Teaching the Faith to Persons Who Have Heard It All Before.* Nashville: Abingdon, 1986.

Crites, Stephen. "The Narrative Quality of Experience." 1971. In Hauerwas and Jones, *Why Narrative?*, 65–88.

Crossan, John Dominic. *The Dark Interval: Towards a Theology of Story.* Sonoma, CA: Polebridge, 1988.

———. *The Power of Parable: How Fiction by Jesus Became Fiction about Jesus.* San Francisco: HarperOne, 2012.

Daniel, Lillian. *Tell It like It Is: Reclaiming the Practice of Testimony.* Herndon, VA: Alban Institute, 2006.

Denning, Stephen. *The Leader's Guide to Storytelling: Mastering the Art and Discipline of Business Narrative.* 2nd ed. San Francisco: Jossey-Bass, 2011.

Fowler, James F. *Stages of Faith: The Psychology of Human Development and the Quest for Meaning.* San Francisco: HarperCollins, 1981.

Gafney, Wilda C. *Womanist Midrash: A Reintroduction to the Women of the Torah and the Throne.* Louisville: Westminster John Knox, 2017.

Gladding, Sean. *The Story of God, the Story of Us.* Downers Grove, IL: InterVarsity, 2010.

Godin, Seth. *All Marketers Are Liars: The Underground Classic That Explains How Marketing Really Works—and Why Authenticity Is the Best Marketing of All.* New York: Portfolio/Penguin, 2012.

Good, James I. "The German Reformed Church in Colonial America." RCUS, April 4, 2009. http://www.rcus.org/reformed-colonial/.

Gottschall, Jonathan. *The Storytelling Animal: How Stories Make Us Human.* Read by Kris Koscheski. New York: Houghton Mifflin Harcourt, 2012. Audiobook.

Groome, Thomas. *Christian Religious Education: Sharing Our Story and Vision.* San Francisco: Jossey-Bass, 1999.

Hammarskjold, Dag. *Markings.* New York: Vintage Spiritual Classics, 2006.

Hauerwas, Stanley, and L. Gregory Jones, eds. "Introduction: Why Narrative?" In Hauerwas and Jones, *Why Narrative?*, 1–18.

———. *Why Narrative? Readings in Narrative Theology.* Eugene, OR: Wipf & Stock, 1997.

Haukenfrers, Norbert. *Fire, Water, and Wind: God's Transformational Narrative—Learning from Narrative Psychology, Neuroscience, and Storytelling about Identity Formation.* Eugene, OR: Wipf & Stock, 2016.

Held Evans, Rachel. *Inspired: Slaying Giants, Walking on Water, and Loving the Bible Again.* Nashville: Nelson, 2018.

Hopewell, James F. *Congregation: Stories and Structures.* Philadelphia: Fortress, 1987.

Hughes, John, dir. *The Breakfast Club*. Universal City, CA: Universal Pictures, 1985. DVD. Universal City, CA: Universal Pictures, 2008.

Humphreys, Keith. "Community Narratives and Personal Stories in Alcoholics Anonymous." *Journal of Community Psychology* 28, no. 5 (2000): 495–506.

Jensen, George H. *Storytelling in Alcoholics Anonymous: A Rhetorical Analysis*. Carbondale: Southern Illinois University Press, 2000.

Jones, Norman L. "Calvinistic Character of the Early German Reformed Church." RCUS, April 4, 2009. http://www.rcus.org/calvinistic -character/.

Kennel-Shank, Celeste. "At Gilead Church in Chicago, Storytelling Is Central to Worship." *Christian Century*, April 9, 2019. https://tinyurl .com/4e8h5rbt.

Kierkegaard, Søren. "The Sickness unto Death." In *A Kierkegaard Anthology*, edited by Robert Bretall, 339–371. Princeton, NJ: Princeton University Press, 1973.

King, Stephen. *The Gunslinger: The Dark Tower I*. Rev. and expanded ed. New York: Signet, 2003.

——. *It*. New York: Signet, 1980.

——. *On Writing: A Memoir of the Craft*. 10th anniversary ed. New York: Scribner, 2010.

Lewis, C. S. *On Stories: And Other Essays on Literature*. New York: Harcourt, 1982.

Lytle, Julie Anne. "Moving Online: Faith Formation in a Digital Age." *Lifelong Faith Journal* 4, no. 1 (Spring 2010): 40–48.

MacIntyre, Alasdair. "Epistemological Crises, Dramatic Narrative, and the Philosophy of Science." In Hauerwas and Jones, *Why Narrative?*, 138–157.

——. "Virtues, the Unity of a Human Life, and the Concept of a Tradition." In Hauerwas and Jones, *Why Narrative?*, 89–110.

McAdams, Dan P. *Stories We Live By: Personal Myths and the Making of the Self*. New York: William Morrow, 1993.

McClintock Fulkerson, Mary, and Marcia W. Mount Shoop. *A Body Broken, a Body Betrayed: Race, Memory, and Eucharist in White-Dominated Churches*. Eugene, OR: Cascade, 2015.

McFague, Sallie. *Metaphorical Theology: Models of God in Religious Language*. Philadelphia: Fortress, 1982.

McFague TeSelle, Sallie. *Speaking in Parables: A Study in Metaphor and Theology*. Philadelphia: Fortress, 1975.

Merritt, Carol Howard. "Net-A-Narratives: The Evolution of the Story in Our Culture, Philosophy, and Faith." In *The Hyphenateds: How*

Emergence Christianity Is Re-traditioning Mainline Practices, edited by Phil Snider, 61–69. St. Louis: Chalice, 2011.

Metz, Johann Baptist. "A Short Apology of Narrative." Translated by David Smith. In Hauerwas and Jones, *Why Narrative?*, 251–262.

Navone, John. *Towards a Theology of Story*. Slough: St. Paul Publications, 1977.

Niebuhr, H. Richard. "The Story of Our Life." In Hauerwas and Jones, *Why Narrative?*, 21–44.

O'Connor, Flannery. *The Complete Stories*. New York: Farrar, Straus and Giroux, 1971.

Oldenburg, Ray. *The Great Good Place: Cafes, Coffee Shops, Bookstores, Bars, Hair Salons and Other Hangouts at the Heart of a Community*. 10th anniversary ed. Cambridge, MA: Da Capo, 1999.

Pagitt, Doug. *Church in the Inventive Age*. Nashville: Abingdon, 2014.

———. *Preaching in the Inventive Age*. Nashville: Abingdon, 2014.

Petersen, Wolfgang, dir. *The NeverEnding Story*. Burbank, CA: Warner Brothers, 1984. DVD. Burbank, CA: Warner Brothers, 2001.

Porter, Thomas. *The Spirit and Art of Conflict Transformation: Creating a Culture of Just Peace*. Nashville: Upper Room, 2010.

Prior, Karen Swallow. *On Reading Well: Finding the Good Life through Great Books*. Grand Rapids, MI: Brazos, 2018.

Rage Against the Machine. "Testify." On *The Battle of Los Angeles*. Recorded 1999. Epic Records.

Ricoeur, Paul. *Time and Narrative*. Translated by Kathleen McLaughlin and David Pellauer. Vol. 1. Chicago: University of Chicago, 1984.

Rohr, Richard. *Breathing under Water: Spirituality and the Twelve Steps*. Cincinnati: Franciscan Media, 2011.

Salmon, Christian. *Storytelling: Bewitching the Modern Mind*. Translated by David Macey. New York: Verso, 2010.

Sessoms, Rick, with Tim Brannagan. *Leading with Story: Cultivating Christ-Centered Leaders in a Storycentric Generation*. Pasadena, CA: William Carey Library, 2016.

Simmons, Annette. *The Story Factor: Inspiration, Influence, and Persuasion through the Art of Storytelling*. 2nd ed. New York: Basic Books, 2006.

———. *Whoever Tells the Best Story Wins: How to Use Your Own Stories to Communicate with Power and Impact*. 2nd ed. New York: Amacom, 2015.

Sweet, Leonard. *From Tablet to Table: Where Community Is Found and Identity Is Formed*. Colorado Springs: NavPress, 2014.

Turk, Evan. *The Storyteller*. New York: Atheneum Books for Young Readers, 2016.

Vann, Jane Rogers. *Gathered before God: Worship-Centered Church Renewal.* Louisville: Westminster John Knox, 2004.

W., Bill. *Twelve Steps and Twelve Traditions.* New York: Alcoholics Anonymous World Services, 1984.

Warner, Rex, trans. *The Confessions of Saint Augustine.* Bk. 11, chap. 20. New York: Signet Classic, 2001.

Wilde, Caleb. *Confessions of a Funeral Director: How the Business of Death Saved My Life.* New York: HarperOne, 2017.

Wimberly, Anne E. Streaty. *Soul Stories: African American Christian Education.* 2nd ed. Nashville: Abingdon, 2005.

Index